Copyright © 2023 by Katheleen Daigle

All rights reserved. This book or any portion thereof may not be reproduced or used in any manner whatsoever without the express written permission of the publisher except for the use of brief quotations in a book review.

Printed in the United States of America

First Printing, 2023

ISBN: 979-8-218-21884-3

www.horsekonfidence.com

Horse Konfidence

Tools to improve your life through an animal communicator's journey

Katheleen Daigle

To my parents and my daughter.

To all the people and animals that crossed my path and played a role to make me the person I am today.

To you who wants a better life, a better connection with yourself and your animals.

Acknowledgments

First and foremost, I would first like to thank YOU, who holds this book in your hands. I hope that my journey and words will help you overcome your own limitations and help you fully live your life as the extraordinary being that you are!

I have been wanting to thank many people for a long time, but I didn't know where to start. I thank God, the Universe, the source of Everything. Without my faith, the beings, and the events that God has placed on my path, none of this would be possible.

Next, I want to thank my parents, Alma & Gilles. You have always been there for me no matter what my choices were. You have always believed in me and been a great support in every way possible. I will forever be grateful for all the values that you have transmitted to me, passion, entrepreneurship, faith, openness, love of animals, mutual aid, respect, and love.

I would like to thank all the mentors, therapists, and authors for the joy of receiving their expertise. I am grateful for their openness to sharing their knowledge in order to help me connect with my soul more, fulfill myself, and simply be the person I am today.

There is also my family, my brothers, my friends from Quebec, and all those who have traveled with me, encouraging me in my various projects... Many of you have spent hours on the phone with me. Sometimes, just knowing that there is always someone there for you is an incredible benefit, something to be grateful for. Jany & Fred, Pierre & Anne-Marie, Katherine G., Josée Sylvain, Catherine L., Lucie and, last but not least, Kathleen L. Thank you for your 30 years of friendship, Kathleen, for our conversations, and our exchanges. I hold them all very dear to my heart. Stephanie, thank you for your friendship, your knowledge, and also for always pushing me out of my limits and helping me carry out this project by finding the perfect team. Sonia, my friend from France, since day one you help me to connect better with my soul and I feel that I know you forever.

To my friends and family from Texas, so many of you have welcomed me, encouraged me, and supported me. I am still a little speechless and proud to now call Texas my home. Kim Matthews and family, Kindyl Scruggs, Ryan Reynolds, Emilie Veillette, Erica Rayer, Piper and Justin Craft, Connie Frey Boe and family, Angie and Paris Jean, Emily Efurd, Brandon Cullins, Madison Wolff, Amber Manley and all trainers, vets, specialists who have agreed to be a part of my projects, thank you. This project would have been hard to accomplish without all of you. Dustin Angelle and Clay Espey, thank you for your friendship, and your openness to work with me. The times spent together, and our nights out have made me so happy. Missy Jean Etheridge and her family... Thank you for introducing me to how fun cutting is, for being who you are, for your friendship, and for being there for me. Whitney and Cole Davison, for welcoming me into your family with open arms. Vicky and Ben Gouin, my American Quebecers, thank you for all the conversations, and our exchanges. Matt Mathews, for the wonderful photos but, especially, for your friendship (anyway;). Tasha and Brian Welsh for welcoming me into your family. Tasha, thank for allowing me to create projects together, for your help, and for taking me everywhere with you.

My daughter, Alexandra Daigle, I am honored to be your mother. I have grown with you as much as you've grown with me. All our memories and shared moments are a part of the woman I am today. This book project would not have seen the light of day if it wasn't for your help and the help of your boyfriend, Logan Patterson, and I'll be forever grateful for that.

Then to finish, there are all the animals and their owners. Thank you for giving me the incredible chance to communicate with them and learn from them. I feel so privileged to be able to work with these wonderful beings.

Thank you! Thank you! Thank you! More of this!

Contents

Introduction 1

PART 1 The story of an animal communicator 3

    Feeling different 5

    Working with people 23

    Working with animals 33

    Say it out loud! 49

    Second trip 61

PART 2 Life's tools 79

    Train yourself, like you train horses 81

    Tool #1 - What are your goals? 85

    Tool #2 - Ask, listen 91

    Tool #3 - Make a choice and take action 97

    Tool #4 - Destroy your fears 103

    Tool #5 - Be Present 109

Tool #6 - Breathe and smile 115

Tool #7 - Take care of yourself 119

Tool #8 - Take a step back 125

Tool #9 - Gratitude 129

Tool #10 - Have faith and enjoy 133

Straight From the horse's mouth 137

Some remarkable communications 147

It's just the beginning… 159

Testimonials 161

FREE GIFT 165

About the Author 167

Introduction

I don't consider myself special. I'm just like everyone else. I am very sensitive to energies, and I am able to communicate with animals.

I decided to write this book to share my experiences and knowledge. My goal is not only to share my story, but, also, to take you through my journey, the animals that allowed me to be who I am today, and what I learned from them. I also wish to share the tools I use for myself, to build the life I want, and how you can do it too.

I would especially like to express how happy I am to be alive today, to be able to appreciate every moment of my life - the good ones and the bad ones - and more importantly, to come out of all of them positively transformed and fulfilled. I don't want to portray that I'm entirely correct. For me, nothing is good or bad. It's only about what we decide to do with what happens in our life. I do not fail, I learn from every moment that life brings me, to feel even more connected with who I really am, and to appreciate this incredible journey called life.

Horse Konfidence

This book is written in two parts. First, you'll discover my journey, so you can better understand where I come from, and where I'm going! In the second part, I'll share with you the tools I use every day to build my dream life, so you can try them for yourself.

Throughout the pages, you will see me use the word "God" and for me, it means "Something bigger than us". Feel free to replace it with Source, Universe, or any other word that better suits you.

If I can only help one person or one animal with these pages, my goal will be achieved.

PART 1
The story of an animal communicator

Chapter 1

Feeling different

> "It is not our differences that divide us. It is our inability to recognize, celebrate, and accept those differences"
> Audre Lorde

Let's rewind a few (many) years and start from my beginning. I was born in Thetford Mines, Quebec, the only province in Canada where French is the main and pretty much the only language. My mom, Alma, enjoyed a first and healthy pregnancy while they were building the house that would raise three children and make countless beautiful memories. As soon as I tried to make my way into this world, though, things got complicated. After long hours of labor, the doctors had to use forceps and an excessive amount of strength to complete the delivery. Unfortunately, what no one knew at the time was that it had severely damaged my spine and nervous system, and it would affect my entire childhood.

My parents both grew up in big families. My dad, Gilles, was the first of 11 kids and my mom was the first of 7. Both growing in the same area, my dad was raised on a small farm where they raised cows and owned a few horses. Whereas, on my mother's side, my grandpa was a miner in the asbestos mines and my grandma sold tissue fabric. My parents were raised to and strongly believe in creating your own path through hard work and dedication. They followed this path and made very successful entrepreneurs. From very early on in their marriage, they both supported each other to build their own businesses. They have never been the lovey-dovey kind, but you can see the love they have for each other through their endless support for each other's' crazy ideas, plans and adventures. They have always pushed us to put all our

Feeling different

energy towards what we are really passionate about, which is what they also did. My dad built a very successful excavation company, and my mom helped him manage the accounts and do all the paperwork. He excelled with any kind of heavy machinery you would give him. No projects were too small or too big, he always did the best work and loved to do it. To this day, even after "retirement", you will find him on a tractor, or a backhoe every chance he gets. My mom was a very talented hairdresser, and really wanted to own her own salon, so my dad built her one in the house. Her business was very successful, and everyone loved her work. She, then, went on to upgrade it to a beauty salon. On top of that, she still always took care of my dad's business's paperwork; she can do it all. Every customer from both businesses loved her, she always welcomed them with a smile and would do anything she could to give them the best service.

They all treated her with the utmost respect, but also knew, you don't mess with Alma! Our house was always crowded with customers coming in and out and the phone was always ringing, but even through the chaos, my parents never made us feel left behind. They worked endless hours, but always included us in the business or made sure to spend time with us. We had a strong sense of closeness in our family, we always made sure to be there for each other when needed. This is something that is really important to all of us, and I am happy my parents passed it down to us. They taught me to be a very good listener, and I became very empathic because of it.

One of my favorite memories from my childhood was something we'd do every Sunday. After church, we would get in the car and drive around, visit some of our family, or we would go check out

Feeling different

some of dad's machinery. As the sun would shine on my face and I closed my eyes to fully soak it in, I would feel so happy to get to enjoy this time with my family. We would end the day with a hearty dinner, the table covered with numerous simple, yet mouth-watering dishes. Sunday dinners were meant to remind us that no matter what happens, no matter how hard the day is, we'll always be together at the end of the day. I have been very fortunate to experience such closeness and solidarity with my family. The family love was not limited to my siblings and parents but extended far beyond. Frequent visits to my grandparents, aunts, and uncles are proof that our family was very close. I learned that one can get through any hard situation if they have their family's support. My maternal Grandparents were my Godparents too, another reason why I was exceptionally attached to them. Grandpa Pouliot, mom's dad, taught me fishing. We would often go to the lake near us to catch some fish, and as we waited for the fish to catch the bait, I would pelt him with question after question. The simple, never-ending questions that every youngster MUST pester their elders with. He would never really entertain my gazillion questions, though, opting to bask in the peace of nature. That's how I learned to enjoy the present moment.

My grandpa Pouliot also loved hockey, and I used to sit with him and watch entire hockey games. I loved how intently he would watch the screen as the puck came near the goal. My grandma Pouliot introduced me to bingo and the game of cards. Now, one would think that this is a boring game meant for the elderly, but it was one of the most amazing times I spent with her.

Horse Konfidence

Summers were one of the most memorable times we shared as a family, as my paternal side visited the family cottage. A small blue lake was built next to the cottages, surrounded by tall, green trees, where my cousins and I would dive in, and we would often play with our ponies together. The nights were mostly spent around the campfire, huddling in blankets as it grew cold at night. Someone would randomly start singing, and eventually, we would all join in.

Feeling different

Because of the complications at my birth, I had a childhood where I was mostly sick with an extremely weak immune system. This meant that I had to abstain from going to school, especially in the early stages of my life. I did, however, attend the first three years of elementary school while I was homeschooled part-time. I returned to school full time when I got to high school. Since most of my time was spent at home, playing with toys or animals, my childhood days were a bit lonely. I did have a few neighborhood friends, but because of my fragile health, I wasn't allowed to play with them. I did have some friends, and some were invisible ones. Growing up, I always felt different. Conforming to the norms of my surroundings wasn't something that appealed to me. I could hear a greater, more purposeful voice surrounding me. I could feel there was more, something greater than what I was shown and more even than what appeared to others. I spent most of my time by myself, but I wasn't entirely alone. I even looked physically different, or maybe I was convinced to believe that I was. I was always set apart from my family, all my cousins have crystal blue or green eyes, and I, on the other hand, was the only one with brown eyes. Too mainstream, too ordinary. I remember being teased by them. They said I was different and that I didn't belong. Perhaps, their intention wasn't so bad. However, I was a simple and fragile child, too naive for the tricks of the world. All of that made me feel a bit marginalized. Some might think it's only my imagination, but now that I look back, I am a firm believer that I had angels and energies around me, ones which were not felt by others. For others, the idea that I could speak and play with people who they couldn't see, or feel was strange, to say the least. However, it decreased my loneliness to an extent. Then again, perhaps, I wasn't so alone after all. I always had animals, angels, and spirits around me.

When I was 4 years old, my mother was baking a cake while I helped by passing her the ingredients. Since my hands did not reach the counter then, I stood on a chair next to her. Mother was focused on whisking the batter when she asked me to pass the baking powder. Instead, she heard a loud thud followed by the creaking of the stool. She turned around to scold me, thinking that I had thrown something on the floor. However, to her utter disbelief, she found me unconscious on the floor. My parents went into a panic, as any normal parents would, and took me to the doctor. At first, they thought that I had only lost balance on the chair which made me fall down. Nevertheless, it was the first of many episodes to happen. Sometimes I would be walking happily, and suddenly I would crash to the ground. After it kept happening continuously, my parents decided to take me to the hospital so that they could run tests and get to the root of the problem. The doctors thought I might have epilepsy and ran numerous brain tests, but the tests did not suggest any such indication. The point to be noted was that I had first lost consciousness and then fallen down, not the other way around. The episodes increased, and no medicine was having any positive effect on me. I was growing weaker and weaker by the day. Some days, I barely had the energy to walk. Because of my low immunity, I was getting prone to diseases easily. People say you

Feeling different

catch chicken pox and mumps only once, and you're good to go after that. What they don't tell you is that if you do catch it a second time, it's way more awful than the first one! I got mumps innumerable times, to the extent that I stopped counting after a while. I have suffered from pneumonia twice, and I have also had the pleasure of catching scarlet fever, measles, and mononucleosis. Oh, and let's not forget, chicken pox visited me a second time, too! And let me tell you, it's no fun being covered with pimples all over, wanting to scratch them so badly when that's the major thing you're not allowed to do.

The medicines prescribed by the doctor never affected me positively, since I was allergic to a lot of them. For this purpose, grandad Pouliot used to prepare homemade medicine by using leaves and roots to find a source of remedy for me. He was very inspired by indigenous peoples, and he would always find the plants which were able to cure me. Even though this medicine helped a little bit, I still wasn't okay. Later at the age of 6, when I was not getting any better, my mother took me to the famous children's hospital, St-Justine Hospital in Montreal. We stayed there for a week with my aunt while the doctors ran more tests on me. Finally, when they couldn't find the fundamental cause of my illnesses, they suggested taking some lymph nodes out and testing them. What they told us later was that I may have cancer and wouldn't be able to walk by the time I reached the age of 18. Of course, this broke my mother's heart. What parent can ever hear that their child would be in so much pain? However, being the strong woman that she is, she refused to accept it. My parents contacted a chiropractor and discussed every detail regarding my health with him. The chiropractor created a special diet for me which I was supposed to follow diligently. The diet included a lot of essential vitamins which I was required to take. I would visit him at least twice a week, in addition to some unpredictable times when I would have a fever or any other symptoms. During these times, my parents drove an hour to take me to the chiropractor just so I could feel better.

At that crucial stage of my life, my parents made an important decision; to stay with me and to believe in me. They had faith that with the proper care and treatment I could get better. They took a bold step to experiment with unorthodox practices which doctors might not have recommended. They are the sole reason that I am able to write this book for you. If it hadn't been for their unfailing belief in me and the Divine, this would not be happening.

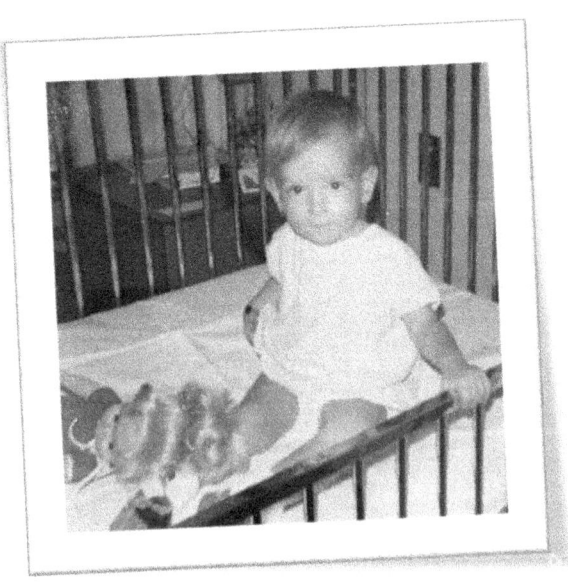

Feeling different

What I have realized later on is that you have to make sure that people or their limitations do not define you. We are often programmed to have limitations in our childhood by our education or people around us constantly telling us how we need to be within certain boundaries. These limits prohibit us from achieving our goals and connecting with ourselves more. But I have learned that we can destroy these limiting boundaries and create our own to serve us on our paths. You must defy all odds, fight with fire till your last breath, and rise above the ashes.

Because of my fragile physique, I was unable to take part in most sports. I was quite interested in music and let myself get carried away with melody. To develop my music skills more, I started learning the violin when I was 7 and kept playing it until I was 16. Now that I think about it, my parents must have been extremely annoyed by my constant playing!

Horse Konfidence

We also always had ponies and horses around. Whenever I would ride a horse or just touch one, I could feel a deep connection. It was as if I could understand them, and they could understand me. I realized that I connected with horses more than I was able to with people. Once, when I was 7, I was riding a beautiful brown pony. Since I wasn't very experimented at the time, I fell down and fractured my elbow. Even though I was crying out in pain, I did not let it discourage me from being closer to animals.

The best way I can explain my profound association with horses is through this anecdote. Dad once brought a pony to my grandparent's farm, so I could try it. What I saw was a beautiful palomino gelding. Its shiny golden hair sparking under the sun made me feel excited to ride it. However, when I sat on the saddle, I was anything but excited. I was unable to understand

Feeling different

why, at the moment, I was anxious, stressed, and unsettled. I told my dad that I wanted to get off.

'Hey, don't worry. It's okay,' He consoled in his calm voice, 'Just take a few deep breaths.' What he thought was that I was scared of riding, which was not true.

Confused, I kept riding. A little while later, the horse stopped and laid down. I took that as my cue to get off. What I noticed then was that the horse was rolling back and forth, clearly not feeling good. Now that I look back at the experience, I understand that my discomfort while sitting on the horse was not my own. I was merely feeling both the physical and emotional discomfort of the horse.

At the age of 10, I decided to try my luck in other sports since I felt stronger than I used to. I was already figure skating but decided that I should take it to the competition level. As excited

as I was about it, I soon realized that I was not meant for it. I caught mononucleosis, making me unable to perform figure skating correctly. I got very sick again and had to be bedridden for 5-6 weeks. So, I resorted to spending time with the friends in my room; the angels and the people no one else could see.

Finally, visiting the chiropractor twice a week for a long time did bear fruit, and I was able to have a 'normal' life. My parents enrolled me in a private high school, boarding during the week nearly 100 miles from home. I saw that as an opportunity to enhance my social circle and develop skills. But I did not have any friends, and I lacked confidence. I wasn't so great at sports either, but I had to find a way. So, I started asking myself questions, like how I could increase my social skills in school. I realized that one of the best ways to do so was to apply to various committees. I opted for event management in some of these committees, which forced me to interact with a lot of people, developing my social skills and confidence. Now that I think about it, I am amazed at the young version of myself. Even at that age, I had the ability to ask myself questions and seek their answers. I am proud of myself for taking action on what I received when I asked and listened.

Even when I was in high school, I would go back home every weekend to spend some quality time with my family. One Friday night, dad and I left for a drive in the woods to get some sand for his job. Everything was quiet when suddenly we heard the sound of a whiplash while we were parked on a small road, which was strange because there was no wind either. It was…unnatural, not human. Naturally, we got scared and rolled the windows up. My

Feeling different

father drove back with a racing heart. I know I wasn't a little child anymore, but that night, I asked my parents if I could sleep next to them. I had a very weary feeling, and I did not want to be alone. The next day when I woke up, my grandpa Pouliot was extremely sick and taken to the hospital where he died in the afternoon. Dad and I were sure that we felt his spirit the night before in the woods. This was a shocking moment for me as I was so close to him, and it opened my eyes to the spiritual world around us.

During some of those teenage years, mom took me to energy healing workshops which taught me about chakras, Reiki, and meditation. I found myself getting interested in it as I understood that there are various things around us that we cannot see but only feel, and it helped me connect to God on a deeper level. It was different from what the Catholic Church taught me, though. I experimented with meditation, finding what worked for me, and perfecting myself in it. It brought me peace, calm, and tranquility. I could feel myself becoming whole.

My 19th birthday was an overwhelming day for me. Looking around, I realized how grateful I was for having such supportive people around me. I was proud of myself for staying strong and having faith, no matter how physically unfit I was. I had worked on myself all these years, yet I would sometimes feel this urgency of living every single day like my last. When I discussed this with my mother, she told me what the doctors had said about me not being able to walk properly until this age. I learned a very important lesson that day; never let the imposed limitations on you keep you down.

Horse Konfidence

During the summers, my parents often took us to different places where we would take part in trail riding with the horses, and we would spend our nights in tents. I associate a lot of wonderful memories with these events.

Today, I am grateful for the trials of my childhood because they taught me to embrace my uniqueness. It's good to do things differently from the crowd. It's a blessing to not always fit in the mold where everyone else wants you to be. I always felt different from everyone else. It's certainly never been my goal to live my life blending in. I never subscribed to the limitation's others embraced. Having that 'expiration date' placed on me sparked a sense of urgency in my life. We are unaware whether it's tomorrow or twenty years from now. For me, every day is the best day of my life. So, why not enjoy it like one?

When the time came to choose a field of study for college, I was completely clueless. I wasn't particularly interested in college and wanted to start my own business, just like my parents. However, they wanted something better for me and urged me to attend college. They did not get a chance to go to college or university, and it was very important to them that I went, because in their mind, it was the only way to create security in my life. I decided to go over the list of different choices and asked God to lead the way. He answered that I should pursue elementary teaching, and my experience supported it as well.

College was the time when I went full rogue. I had one rule; it's better to do something than to regret not doing it. I was exploring myself, and I used to party until the sun came up. Just like many

Feeling different

college students at the time, I was hooked to rock and roll music. The way the beat and the music hit the soul is unmatchable. I was often found in bars, fell in love, and got my heart broken several times. But I'll tell you what, I don't regret anything at all. I believe myself to be a passionate person and I love with all the conviction I have. My college days were wild and free, full of hope and life. I was glad that I was alive and able to enjoy every blessing that God had bestowed on me.

What remained constant throughout were the horses. Me, my mom and my brothers would still attend competitions every weekend during the summers. Sometimes my dad would join us when he was not working. Whenever I was not working or in school, you could always find me in the barn riding horses. Some mornings were harder than the others because of the partying, but I was young and enjoying life.

Chapter 2

Working with people

After I graduated college and started working as a part-time teacher, I couldn't help but feel discontent. I had always been a grateful person, someone who was always full of life, never giving up. I had always been happy with what I had. And even yet, I gave it my best to be satisfied. However, I felt as if something major was absent from my life. I wanted to do something on my own, start a business which could make me feel content.

How does one feel 'complete'? How does one fill the gaping hole inside their heart, the forever feeling of unfulfillment? It seems as if we spend our entire lives trying to figure out what we want. We roam aimlessly, stumbling here and there, running after one thing then another, to somehow cover the inevitable impending chaos raging inside us, only to end up in the same place we started. It's like a loop.

Every weekend, a popular horse event was taking place in Quebec where my brothers participated. The event included a pick-up race and exchange race. In a pick-up race, a rider rides the horse at full speed around the arena while the rider's teammate runs from the middle of the arena and tries to jump on the horse. An exchange race is similar, however, here, when the second rider jumps on the horse, the first rider jumps off. Because of how dangerous the game is, the participants are often injured. As you can guess, my brothers and other members of my family suffered some injuries. Since I have this natural tendency to help people, along with this ability to understand them, I enrolled myself in a one-year massage therapy course so that I could help them heal.

My teachers were amazed at how quickly and efficiently I was able to learn the various techniques. I immersed myself fully in it and felt like I was totally in my element. I learned about the different holistic ways to support and heal the body. Perhaps, this was what was missing from my life. The feeling of helping people. Immediately after my graduation from the massage therapy school, I started working with my mom's clients in her home salon. I was confident in my skill, and it showed in my work, too. Because of how popular my massage became amongst the clients; I was able to fully develop my own business. I accomplished it. Even though I was still teaching at the same time, I was happy that I had another profession that I was satisfied with, and it made me feel whole. To my utter delight, the business was booming, and my clients were satisfied with the massage therapy I provided. Subsequently, I started noticing

Working with people

something unique. I wasn't able to understand it initially. I felt various emotions when I was working on a client. Sometimes I would feel traumatized, scared, or in fear, as if something unfortunate would happen. Other times, I had feelings of doubt or uncertainty.

After careful consideration and pondering over the situation, I understood that while I was unwinding their knots and easing their pain, what I was able to feel were the emotions of my clients. The most interesting aspect here was that I could also understand which emotion was causing the client pain. At the beginning, I dared not to discuss this with the client. But soon, my curiosity increased, until eventually I started explaining what I had seen or felt while massaging them. Their response was undeniable. They were flabbergasted and intrigued by how I was able to understand their deepest emotions. When I talked about their personal feelings with them, ones which they had kept hidden in the depths of their heart, unable to communicate them to anyone, their reaction varied. While some cried their hearts out, finally relieved that someone was able to understand them, others just laughed it off, still in disbelief of my skills. One thing was for certain; they were overwhelmed. I understood that God had given me a gift; the gift to understand people, to unlock their emotions and memories, which eventually helped them heal, to support them, and to be an aid to them in ways medicine could never.

I gradually became confident in my services and decided to add the emotion discovery part to it. A woman came to me, worried about her obesity. She explained that no matter how many times she lost weight, she would always gain it back. She would lose 40 pounds but end up gaining 60 more. She felt helpless and rejected and did not feel confident in her own skin. When I started working with her, I understood that she had had an abusive childhood, and the trauma was still trapped inside her. Carefully, I talked to her about it. As I talked, and she listened, her eyes started tearing up a little. I put a gentle hand on her shoulder, showing her that I was there for her.

'Oh, Katheleen!' And with this, she burst into tears. I encouraged her to talk about it and explain what she felt, and she did. I am glad that I helped her speak up and let the tension inside her go away. After putting in time and consistent effort with her for a year, we unblocked the trauma and pain inside, and she was successful in losing 60 pounds, which she never gained back. It was as much a success for me as it was for her. That day, I felt fulfilled.

This event boosted my confidence, and I was able to work with more clients. One of my prominent clients had an issue of severe back pain. The pain was to such an extreme that he struggled with walking, a major hindrance in day-to-day life. After one session, I was able to perceive the source of his pain: negative portrayal of self. Perhaps it was his everyday life or the people around him, but he was not happy with himself. I talked to him about what I felt while I worked on his back. He trusted me and we worked on it together. Soon after a few sessions, we were making progress. I helped him release his inner tension, think of himself more positively, and have more faith in himself. This helped him walk with ease. What was interesting about the whole

Working with people

situation was that whenever he resorted back to his own negative self-image, his back pain would return. It was like his body was a thermometer which told him the temperature of his inner environment. His body showed him what needed to change. This is actually the case with every one of us. More often than not, our bodies are reminding us what we need to do for ourselves. However, we are often either too busy or too ignorant to notice it.

I was glad to be the channel through which people were able to heal themselves with issues they were afraid to face alone. I could help clients find their way, but only if they allowed me to. Some of them had blocked their feelings to the extent where they were completely unapproachable. Whether it was their fear of being vulnerable or their skepticism of my practices, they reacted in a negative way, sometimes calling me a witch or a devil. Since this wasn't the first time, I had been called that, I chose to ignore their incessant barbs and just kept going. Nevertheless, their taunts still got to my heart and hurt me. Soon, the pressure became unbearable. With a broken heart, I decided to close my business after six years of successful massage therapy. I was troubled by the fact that even though I was trying my absolute best to help people and perform to the best of my abilities, I wasn't appreciated enough. I was getting more discouraged by the day. I realize now that I wasn't confident of my work because at the time people's opinions and their negative thoughts had a deep effect on me, especially those of my friends and family. At the time, I wasn't strong enough to get past that.

Since I got my confidence shattered by the persistent demeaning remarks regarding my massage practices, and I wasn't confident enough to say, 'I don't care about your comments, I'll continue to do as I please!' I eventually caved into the external pressure. I established that I was good enough to be a teacher. I would blend in, trying to fit into the 'mold' of being 'normal' and I wouldn't have to listen to any more mockery.

Where I should have trusted myself and my abilities, I let fear reside in my heart and stopped offering my massage services to people. But now that I look back, my time after I closed my business was not wasted either. I chose that time to focus on myself more. I sought mentors, read self-improvement books, and took therapy sessions because I wanted to be a better version of myself. I also took many courses about animal communication and energy work to learn how to connect to myself and to transform my limiting beliefs.

The following phase of my life was busy, tough, and excessively exhausting. I gave birth to my beautiful daughter. In due course, my life became about caring for and loving my daughter, caring for my animals and working three jobs to sustain us. Since I was a single mother, I had to have a stable income to make ends meet. Not long after, the overload of work took a toll on me. I felt completely burnt out and lifeless. Without wasting any more time, I went to the director of the school and told him that I realized that I wanted to work to live, not the other way around. The people around me and my family called me crazy for quitting a full-time stable job with great benefits. They said I was being ungrateful. However, I really wanted my freedom back. Even though I didn't know what it was that I wanted the most, I felt that I was destined for greater things, that I had to keep exploring.

My sole focus became my daughter and providing her with a healthy and loving environment. Because I had spent my childhood amongst animals and nature, I wanted my daughter to experience it as well. Hence, I built us a house close to my parent's barn so that she could experience much of what I had loved in my youth. I sold my horses to focus on other aspects of life. However, I never missed a single weekend of competition and went there to have fun with the horses and be immersed in their energy.

I loved having horses around me, to feel their vibrancy, and I wanted my daughter to experience that, too. Thus, my parents gifted her a pony when she was only two so that she could enjoy the joy of riding one. She learned to ride really early and used to ride as fast as the wind (still does)! And me or my mom was always running behind her to take care of her so that she didn't fall!

I put in my best efforts to be a great mother, have a good profession that made me feel satisfied, and stayed close to the horses since they gave me energy while I was constantly working on myself and connecting with myself more. I was perpetually trying to figure out the best plan to achieve my goals. Even if I felt stuck at any point, I did not stop working towards them.

I am a firm believer of the notion that whatever happens, happens for a reason. You CAN learn from your experiences and implement it. No experience is good or bad or 'wasteful'. It's about how you choose to perceive it. You can either stay stuck in your 'bad' phase and keep telling yourself that you're a victim, or you can understand that this is all part of God's plan and grow from it. You must take responsibility for your own actions, no matter if they're good or bad. One major lesson that I learned was that it is nobody else's, but your responsibility to keep you happy. What I was trying to do, perhaps, was to derive my happiness from other people's comments. I was looking for validation in their satisfaction through my work. No one, and I repeat, no one can provide you the love that you need, even if they're your children, your spouse, or your parents. It's unfair to you and others to give them the responsibility of keeping you happy. You need to work for it yourself. I realized that if I wanted to be really happy and satisfied with my own life, I was the only one who could do it. I had to find ways to keep providing me with joy. Others can only motivate you to be better and contribute a certain amount of happiness.

The more you work on yourself, and listen to yourself, the easier it will be for you to connect with your soul. You cleanse yourself, and you allow yourself to breathe. Needless to say, my realization of this simple fact did not mean that I immediately had a better life. I had to put in constant effort. But it was okay; you only need to take one step at a time. I understood that in order to provide my daughter with the love that she needs to nurture, I needed to start with myself.

It's simple; in order to love people, or even animals, unconditionally, you need to fall in love with yourself first.

Horse Konfidence

Because only then will you love them without any expectations. Your sole motive will be only to love them because you won't be trying to fill your voids by their actions and statements which might affect you. Of course, their reciprocation of your love will always be a bonus for you, but it won't be the single most thing helping you survive.

Chapter 3

Working with animals

There was something more to life. There had to be. My life couldn't only involve teaching. I kept feeling that I was destined for something else, something out of the ordinary. Something which teaching could not provide me. Until I found what it was, I kept experimenting with teaching, too. I taught at an elementary school for a couple of years, but soon grew out of it. I couldn't see any growth left there for me. I proceeded towards teaching high school in the hopes of advancing my own personal growth.

Throughout those years, I was a substitute teacher. I was the one they would send to those tough classes where no one else wanted to go or where the teacher had to leave for a couple of weeks to take a break. I thrived with kids who were a little rebellious and wouldn't listen to anyone else. It was a new challenge every time, and I enjoyed that. It was encouraging and lifting for me because

I knew the impact I could make on these young people who may have been written off by everyone else, and I knew I could change their lives.

I saw I had a real impact on them, and it was really gratifying for me. I've had the chance to meet some of my students in their adult life, and they shared how I had an immense impact in the course of their life.

In the final year of my teaching career, I taught Introduction to Computers to seniors and elderly. However, it was not proving to be beneficial for their needs, the classes were not adjusted for their level of understanding. I discussed with the directors regarding a change in the program and offered to do it myself, but they refused due to several reasons. Eventually, I left the school because I was not satisfied with the way I felt; I was not able to help the people the way I wanted to. I did not want to stay in a place where my true potential wasn't recognized or fulfilled. Hence, after 23 years of teaching, I quit my profession and decided that it was time I followed a new passion, something I could strive for. Something that could not only satisfy my basic needs, but also deeply nourish my soul.

I decided to try my luck as an entrepreneur again, using my teaching experience. For my newest venture, I decided I would create a course for elderly people to help them master the use of technology. More and more seniors were struggling with the advancement of technology, and many did not get the support and help needed to understand it from their families and close ones. I devised a plan on how to gain more potential customers.

Working with animals

Each day that I wasn't working, I would go out, explore and talk to at least three people who could be my clients. Within six short months, I got to hire five teachers for my blooming business. And because of the popularity of my business, some entrepreneurs approached me and asked me to help them with their social media. I studied how one can help expand their business through social media, took some classes, did the research, and designed a course for entrepreneurs. That is how I started helping other businesses with their marketing. A very important point I was trying to teach them was the importance of gaining your customers' trust and building credibility. A great way to do that is to give them free advice before they even become your customer. So, once again, I started asking myself questions on how I could help these businesses the most and really show them the importance of giving to receive more customers. Well, what better way than to do it myself. That's when I decided to start Vision Cheval. A Facebook page dedicated to informing the equine community about bits, saddle fit, feed, supplements, hoof care, health, training and much more with the help of trainers and experts in the domain. And all that, for FREE! But I had a bigger motivation behind it all.

As I have talked about before, my whole life I felt like I had a special connection with animals, that I could feel what they were feeling, but at that point in my life is where I really started to understand what I was feeling and really focused on developing that gift. With a lot of focus, breathing exercises, and changes in energy levels I could completely connect with horses and hear what they had to say, and, furthermore, communicate back and forth with them. I could find out what they liked or didn't, but how could I tell people? There's no way they would believe in my skills and trust my interpretation of their horses' personalities, health, likes, dislikes, and much more. That's where creating Vision Cheval came in. Two birds, one stone. I got to show businesses what they could do with this marketing technique in their business, and I got to bring in experts in the equine industry that could educate people about the many subjects that horses would talk to me about. I could create this awareness and bring solutions to these problems horses would talk to me about hoping humans would get to know more and do better for their horses without having to say, "I talk to horses". I kept this my secret, while still trying to help horses. So, I started making these videos and putting them on Facebook, creating a resource bank with opinions and facts from vets, trainers, and other specialists. After 1 year, my videos got over 1,000,000 views, which is quite a lot of attention for a French Facebook page based in Quebec, Canada.

Once I saw how popular these videos could be, I started filming and selling full-length online clinics with professional trainers to help horses and riders. I don't know why this is the direction I took, but I just had a feeling that's what I needed to do and that's how I felt like I could use my gift to the best of my abilities at that time. Looking back, I know it was all part of a bigger plan, God's plan. Have you ever had an idea in mind, and you've got no clue why you had that idea or where it's going, but you just have to follow it? This feeling was so strong I couldn't ignore it. I just had to go with it and see where it took me. Little did I know, it was only the beginning of a way bigger plan, His plan.

Slowly, very slowly, I talked about my ability to communicate with animals with my closest friends and family. I wanted to be able to help them work as a powerful team with their horses. Some were open to it and were thankful for my help, and even though I was careful who I talked to about it, some were very skeptical and thought I was going crazy. Sometimes, they almost convinced me I was going crazy, too, but faith in this amazing gift always kept me going.

Then, there was this one communication. One of my good friends, who I had helped before, had a horse who wasn't performing to the best of his abilities. Her usually very strong, lovely gelding was acting lethargic, lacked appetite, and had no desire to run barrels. She was really worried about her horse, and even though she was confident in my skills, her boyfriend was not. Constantly judging me, he had no faith in my ability; thought it was impossible. I decided not to let his disbelief get to me, and helped her and her horse. I looked at the picture she sent me of the gelding and focused on connecting with him. I started to feel very tired. Suddenly, visions of orange-ish, red liquid filled my mind. Iron, I thought. He's low in iron. I called my friend and told her that I suspected her horse was deficient in iron. As expected, her boyfriend did not believe in us and intended to prove us wrong. He ordered a blood test the same day, while I patiently waited for the results to arrive.

To his amazement, the blood work results, and a vet confirmed that the horse indeed needed more iron. He quickly changed his mind about the communication. They added an iron supplement to his diet and within 2 weeks he was back to running and winning! This was the first time that my conclusions were confirmed by a vet AND a test! This helped my confidence a lot. I told her to not talk about it, I still wasn't ready to share it with the world, but she didn't listen. So someone else called for help. And then another. And another.

It was a bit overwhelming, I was more than happy to help people and their horses, but I had never even thought about doing it as a business or for any money. I saw it as a unique gift, a skill I had, that could help my friends and family and their horses.

The same friend called me a few weeks later, feeling like there was something new bothering her gelding. The iron deficiency was fixed, but the horse still seemed bothered by something. I took a look at the horse and asked him to show me what the issue was. He showed me that his right hip and back were painful; he needed a chiropractic adjustment. But here's what blew me away the most. He said he wanted someone with big hands to work on him. I won't lie, I laughed, thought it was a weird request, but I didn't doubt it and told my friend what he said. When I told my friend, she had about the same reaction I did, but she went to work to find a chiropractor who fit the description. Soon, she sent me a picture of the man she had hired to make the adjustments. The man was 6'2" with exceptionally large hands. He adjusted him and the horse went back to winning right away!

Working with animals

This communication really stood out for me because the horse knew what could help him.

Here's another communication that stood out for me in the beginning. Another friend of mine asked my help with her horse because he wasn't performing well. Two things needed to be fixed, both pretty simple. First thing was that his saddle didn't fit well and was not comfortable at all. Secondly, he wasn't having enough fun. There's no reason why horses shouldn't enjoy their rides every day, too. He did not like to do drills in the arena, that was too boring. He thrived on fun, variety, and excitement. I told her she should change it up. Go ride in the pasture, let him have more fun. Play with him, enjoy the rides. Soon after she made these changes, they became a much better team, improved their times drastically and both enjoyed it a lot more.

I became a tool, a mediator, to help riders and their horses perform better. I was happy to be a part of their team, and to help them achieve their goals.

In October 2017, my mom and I took a retreat with one of our mentors to Riviera Maya in Mexico. It was a beautiful coastal area surrounded by turquoise seas and sandy beaches. Every morning, we sat on the beach with the other participants, meditating, learning, and helping each other work with energies. Being there in that small piece of heaven made me feel really calm. One morning, my mom went back to the room to get something while I was standing in the water next to others while they fed some bread to the fish. I kept my distance from the fish because I wasn't particularly fond of them. Suddenly, I was surrounded by a thousand fish! All I wanted to do was run away as I felt the weird feeling of those fish touching me. I tried to calm myself down by breathing, but it wasn't helping. Panicked, I started crying, bringing my mentor close to me.

'Do you trust me?' She asked, with earnest eyes.

'Yes.' I trembled, as my heart pounded. She told me to stay still and said they were cleaning things off of me. She made me lay down in the water and asked others to come around me and hold me. She said something to calm me down, but I have no idea what it was as I could only focus on controlling my breathing. My mom came back finally. Turns out, as my mom made her way back to the beach, she had lost her way. My mentor finished the energetic work on me and the fish slowly all left. What started as a very emotional experience ended up being very relieving and fun. I felt peaceful, happy, and more connected to myself. I honestly can't explain fully what happened that day. But I believe that God sent those fish towards me so that I could have more faith in myself and build a stronger connection with myself and Him.

That night, we made a reservation at the hotel's restaurant. It was a Texas themed steakhouse, something that I love to eat! 9 of us were supposed to eat together, but nobody else showed up, it was just me and my mom. As I sat down and looked around my surroundings, I felt emotional for some reason. Within a few moments, I had difficulty breathing and was trying hard to catch my breath. My mom looked at me, worried, and asked me what was going on. I took a moment and then answered, 'I feel like home.' Confused, she asked me to explain. I told her that I had thought that I might leave Quebec, my loving home, for Oklahoma with my daughter, but I had never thought about moving to Texas. Of course, I didn't understand it then, but I was meant to go there. This incident took place a year before I moved to Texas.

In December of 2017, I, along with a few friends of mine, went to the much-awaited National Finals Rodeo in Las Vegas, something which we had been planning for six months. Vegas was very entertaining; we went to the rodeo, shopped a lot, and traveled around the city visiting landmarks. One afternoon, we were all relaxing and talking in the bedroom when I voiced out that I had a feeling that I would be coming here again one day, for a bigger purpose. I had no idea how or why, but I knew I would be back.

About a month prior to my trip in Las Vegas, I broadened my online clinics with Vision Cheval and filmed one with a jumper

horses' trainer. This was a side of the horse world I didn't know much about but found very interesting and loved the experience. On December 22nd, to my astonishment, one of the jumper trainers asked me to travel to Ocala, Florida, to make more educational videos. I was beyond honored to be asked to work with them. Florida! The opportunity was mind blowing! All I needed was a trailer with living quarters and a truck, and I could be on my way to the opportunity of a lifetime. I had wanted to expand my mind, get more exposure, and there it was! Then what was tying me down? I was recently out of a relationship, and my daughter had just moved out. If anything, I could use this time to focus on myself more. I had nothing to hold me back.

There were two issues, though. One, I didn't own a trailer with living quarters. And second, I didn't have a truck either which could pull said trailer. I only owned a Honda Civic. That night, I prayed to God wholeheartedly.

'God, if this is the right thing for me to do, please provide me with everything I need to make this trip.'

It was as if God was only waiting for me to ask Him and already had His resources pooled and ready.

The very next day, my cousin called and asked me for help with his computer. I was more than happy to go help him, but it also gave me an idea. I asked him if, in return, I could borrow his trailer for the winter. I told him about my project, and he said 'Sure, with the snow, I can't use it anyway.' It worked out perfectly.

I went to visit my parents and told them about my upcoming project. I was thinking of asking one of my uncles if I could borrow his truck. But before that, my dad offered me to take his, in return for my car while I was gone.

'Why not? Works for both of us!' I said and clapped my hands in delight.

Horse Konfidence

God made things easier for me. I only had to ask Him once to help me, and He did. I believe that if you want something with full conviction and work for it, you will never be turned away from it. And that is exactly what happened for me. God already has everything planned out and if He wants you somewhere, he will make it happen.

While I was getting ready to leave at the beginning of February 2018, we got a splendid offer on our house. I was ecstatic. It seemed like the right thing to do; I could use this time to understand where I wanted to go in my life. Sure, I wouldn't own a place when I came back to Canada, but my parents have this amazing little loft on the second floor of our barn, and it would be just fine for me when I returned. I set out on my adventure hauling two horses for my friend, who agreed to split the fuel cost with me. It was a 24-hour drive from Thetford Mines to Ocala. I was on the road, and I felt free. This was all God's plan. The way everything fell in place was not in my control, but all in His. That was His plan. There's always a plan and a reason, never doubt it.

The first twenty-two hours went smoothly, while the last two came with obstacles. About 150 miles from my destination, I heard a loud 'clunk!' from the trailer. I pulled over to assess the situation, one of the axles had broken. I called my friend to come get her horses. Going pretty slow, I reached the destination on three wheels. Those few hours felt longer than the whole rest of the trip. Tired and bedraggled but thrilled to finally be there, I made it! However, my trailer was not in hauling shape, and I had to get it fixed as soon as possible. When I asked around the next

Working with animals

day, I found out that all the repair shops were about a month out to get any appointment.

I did not let that worry me, and I set out to do what I had come here for. I was in my element, making videos about horses. The trainer was very welcoming and helped me understand those horses, their jobs, and the discipline itself.

Two weeks later, I still hadn't found someone to fix my trailer. I decided to take 2 days off to visit a friend, the mentor with whom I had gone on the retreat to Mexico, and her husband in Fort Pierce. They were selling their house and needed help sorting paperwork. Meeting them was very refreshing as we talked about life, energy, motivation, and everything in between. They chose to take me to a steakhouse for dinner as they were aware about my love for steak. On the way there, she gave me one of the best advices I've ever received in my life. First, she asked me what I really wanted from life. It took me what seems like forever to even think about something to say, but to be honest, I didn't have a clear answer to that. At the moment, I was just going with the flow. I knew that buying a house and staying permanently in one place wasn't my cup of tea anymore. I got this taste of the free life on the road and got addicted to it. As I said, I found out that I wanted to go from adventure to adventure, wherever I wanted, whenever I wanted. As I kept talking, I was finding answers to my own questions. I said that I would be content with a living quarters trailer, a truck, and a small storage to store my supplies. I would love to work in an environment where distance doesn't matter, where I am able to spread my voice across borders and have an impact on the world. Then came THE advice.

'It's time to plant the seed in the ground, and let it grow.' She said calmly and softly.

Ok. Now I was confused. Plant what seed?

She explained, "It's simple. You put your dreams in the ground just like a seed, trust the process, and wait for it to grow. You water the seed daily. If you plant a carrot seed one day, you water it and wait for it to mature, waiting for the perfect time for it to be harvested. You know that you will get your carrots the way you expect them. Bringing your dreams to life is a similar process. When you really want something, you ask for it. Don't be afraid to be really precise on what you ask for. You don't stop yourself from dreaming big, and you shouldn't. When you put your dreams in the ground, you don't ask for it again. Instead, you are thankful for it every single day as if you already have it. And I always say 'Thank you, and more of this' when I receive something. This thankfulness and gratitude are similar to watering your plant. The more thankful you are, the quicker you will be bestowed with what you want. It's as simple as that!"

And so I planted my first seed. My work. I didn't know what exactly I wanted to do, but I knew what I wanted out of it. And I put it in the ground (in my heart). Then I asked for my own truck and trailer, and for storage for all my belongings. Until then, I had this trailer in Florida, and the loft when I made it back home and that was the only sense of security I needed, a roof over my head. So, I planted all my seeds, then I started thanking God for all of it. Not just being thankful but feeling thankful from my very core. There's a big difference between those two. Now, I had to trust the process. Not try to control the how, when, or what, just put the seed in the ground and let God and life bring it to you in its time. So that's what I did.

I went back to Ocala, feeling I had learned something very important on my short trip. I added a lot of new tools to my toolbox.

A few days later, the city was hit by an enormous storm, which caused an electricity shortage. There was no internet for several days, even the phone service was down for a bit. I couldn't even make any videos; it was too windy. I had nothing to do, the trailer suddenly felt very small, and I was starting to feel a little depressed. I still hadn't found anyone to fix the axle, so I couldn't go home either. I decided to go to Starbucks where I could get internet access. I contacted a friend who does Tarot readings. She called me right away. She listened patiently, as I explained what was going on. After getting my story of woes and worries off my chest, her reply was simple, as if she knew all along what I had to do.

'It's time, Katheleen.' She said with a small smile on her face.

'Time...for what exactly?' I asked, perplexed, making her laugh.

'You don't even know it?! My dear, it's time for you to tell the world about your gift of communicating with animals! I've been telling you that for a while!' She exclaimed.

'What? No! I am not going to do that.'

'What do you have to lose?' She asked rhetorically, spreading her arms. When I thought about it, I really did have nothing to lose. I was stuck in my trailer with nothing but time on my hands. I didn't want fear to stop me from doing something that I was meant to do. I took a deep breath and let it out slowly.

'Okay, let's do it!'

Chapter 4

Say it out loud!

'I can communicate with animals.'

'I have been doing it for friends and family, and now I'm offering it to all of you. If you would like me to talk to your horses, send me your horse's picture, three questions you have for/related to them, and your phone number on Messenger. I'll call you back. You can pay what you want, there's no set price.' March 15, 2018.

That's it. Simple.

I asked God to show me if this was the right thing to do. I mentally sorted through my fears, and I knew I didn't want them to hold me back anymore. I stared at the words I'd typed on my Facebook feed. I eventually said 'no more' to my fears and doubts and published it. No going back now.

Five minutes passed, then ten. Likes and comments started racking up on the post. In no time, it had over thirty shares! Less than thirty minutes later, requests for communication were pouring into my inbox. They started in a trickle, then a stream, followed by a flood! I had over a hundred requests within the next few days.

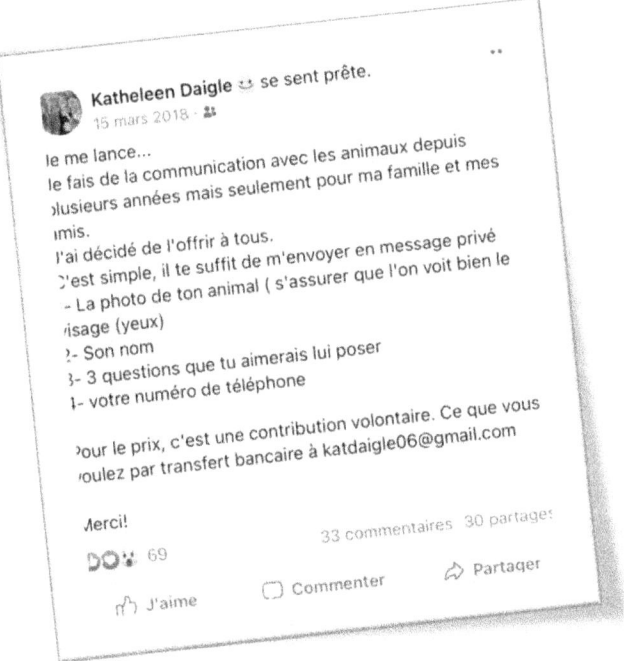

I was shocked and thrilled at the same time. I didn't sleep much that week, I just wanted to talk to all these horses. Not to mention that there was still no internet due to the thunderstorm. Hence, I spent a better part of that week in McDonald's parking lot communicating with animals. The whole experience was exhilarating! It felt great to be able to help so many people and horses!

Within a few days, the storm ended, the sun was shining, and the internet came back. I was even able to get the trailer's axle fixed too! I decided to go back home on March 25.

I thanked God immensely for all the blessings and felt in my heart that it was all His plan. If all of these unfortunate events hadn't happened, the broken axle and the storm, I wouldn't be where I am now, and I wouldn't be writing this story.

It's important to take a step back in life. Periodically, I make sure to step back and allow myself to look at things from a different perspective so that I can expand my mind. What's important to realize is that nothing is good or bad in itself. In fact, it's more about what you do with that situation and what you learn from it. Don't self-victimize when something unlucky happens. If you dwell in self-pity, wondering "why me", "Why did this happen to me?" or "What did I do to deserve this?", you won't be able to see the bigger picture. I always ask myself questions such as "What's blocking me from advancing forward?", "What can I learn from this?", "What can I change?", and "What kind of energy can I be?".

A new start.

As I got home, I discussed my plan with my parents. I was residing in their loft, while beginning the process of looking to buy a truck, a trailer, and a storage container. Every night, I thanked the Universe and God for the things that I wanted, as if I had already gotten them, just like my friend had advised me. Every Sunday, I would dance a little to show my gratitude and joy, just to make sure that the Universe knew and understood how those things would create a life full of happiness and make my soul realize this was meant to be.

As the demand for communication with animals kept increasing, my mom hired an accountant for me to make sure that my business was legal. Initially, the accountant laughed it off, insinuating that I wouldn't be making enough money for the government to notice.

About a month later, he took a second look at how much I was making.

'Woah, there! We might have to change some things!' He chuckled. And so I started charging sales tax, which was required for a business in Canada.

Suddenly, everything I'd envisioned and desired started working out in my favor like magic! The stars had finally started to align, I could see my dreams coming to life, and all my hard work paying off. My parents agreed that I could stay in the loft, so I bought a container to store my belongings. I was delighted. I had a job that allowed me to travel the world and to be with horses. More importantly, after feeling like an outcast my entire life, feeling as if I was different, I ultimately found the path for me, allowing me to be my unapologetic self and find peace in helping the animals.

During that summer, we signed the paperwork to sell the house, which finally allowed me to pull the trigger on buying a trailer. I still hadn't found the one for me, but only 14 days later, I found one I really liked. Turns out, it had been online for over 2 months, but I never saw it. Proof that you can't control when something

Say it out loud!

is supposed to happen in your life, and that opportunities WILL find you when you're ready. I just kept being thankful for all the blessings, and the more life showed me these signs, the more I became attentive to them, and the more signs I received. God has every detail planned, and he will help you achieve your goals in the right time. God has a lot of ways to bring small and big moments of joy in your life.

My mom decided to join me to go look at the trailer. It was in Niagara Falls, Ontario, about a 9-hour drive from our house. During the journey, she shared her and dad's concerns about me getting involved in a personal financial crisis if I bought the horse trailer and because I didn't have a truck, just a car. My daughter was still studying in College in Oklahoma, and they were aware of the money I had spent to help her and how important it was to me. I listened to her concerns but chose not to say anything. She's my mom. She's allowed to be worried. I wanted to stop for dinner at a decent restaurant on the way, but she insisted that we drive straight to the hotel. I now know that it was because she didn't want me to spend too much money. We had to find a hotel soon because it was getting very late. The first two that we passed by were too expensive for her. My mom searched through the internet to find a cheaper one, and she eventually did. I quietly drove there, but it seemed creepy, so I turned back and went back to the first one. By this time, I was angry, not at my mom, but at myself. I decided to speak up.

'Mom, I am sorry, but I am mad right now. Not at you, but at myself, because I am letting your fears affect me. I understand that you're my parent, and it's your duty to be worried about me, but I learnt a lot when I went to Florida. I have worked a lot on destroying the programming and fears that have kept me away from my goals. One of them was money. I was always told to believe that earning money is hard, and if it's easy then it must be sketchy or there is something wrong with the way it is being earned.' I couldn't stop from expressing myself, and I didn't want to. I've always been close to my mom, and I didn't like the feeling of limitation, so I felt like she needed to know what I understood of life. 'I always let myself be limited by scarcity, and it's stopped me from achieving goals. I realized that this was hindering me from getting closer to many goals. So now, I have instilled in my mind that money is easy to make, it's free flowing, it brings me joy, and I will have plenty in my life. I believe that this is true, and I have faith in it. I know that God is using this event and you to test me to see if I really believe in it or not. And instead of enjoying this trip as a mother-daughter duo, I let your fears of money shortage affect me, preventing us from making the most of it. So now, we're gonna turn back, go to that nice, comfy hotel, and enjoy our trip because we deserve it. I am convinced that everything will turn out just fine.' I was happy to have let it all out. I quickly glanced at my mom to see her reaction and realized that she actually seemed relieved to hear this. She nodded and we resumed our journey in peace.

The next day, we examined the trailer, and I noticed that I was getting much more than I had expected, more than the seed that I had planted in my heart! The trailer was luxurious, with a fancy interior, and considering the amount of money I paid, it was magnificent! I was so thankful to the Universe and God and allowed myself to feel the joy too. To celebrate my happiness on the matter, Mom and I went for a delicious dinner, which we had in the trailer that night. The moment was not only enjoyable because I had bought a trailer, but also because I made memories with my mom.

The next month, I bought a brand-new truck and named it Thor. I was adamant that I would have the opportunity to travel the world with it. My animal communication business was booming, hence I decided not to take any more contracts regarding helping others with social media and computer-related concerns. I kept working on Vision Cheval, my own business related to the horse world.

One day, I received a text message from a barrel racer from Arkansas who was having trouble with her mare but was unable to point-out the reason. One of my friends gave her my number while she was in Quebec. I was about to call her after I communicated with her mare, but there was an issue. I was barely able to speak English at the time. However, I did not let that discourage me and sought help from Google Translate and got pictures of the horses' parts with English labels to convey what I had found. I let go of my fears and decided to just do it. My goal was only to help the mare. I am extremely thankful to her for showing such patience with me, because it helped open numerous doors for my business after she shared my phone number with her peers. Just like a snowball rolling down a mountain, my business grew every day. I was full-time now and got the chance to work with a lot of girls and amazing horses rodeoing in Quebec from the USA. I had the chance to work with amazing horses before, but to work with girls coming from the USA; I had never expected that!

God was constantly moving me towards my goals, my destination. The first American rider suggested that I attend the Barrel Futurities of America (BFA) in Oklahoma City, for which I got extremely excited. Not only because of the BFA, but also because my daughter was studying in college very near there, and I missed her dearly. Thus, I asked around in Quebec if anyone was interested in co-piloting. But before any plans for Oklahoma could be made, God had other plans for me.

In September 2018, I attended a Tony Robbins conference in Ottawa, Ontario, with my friend who had convinced me to share my gift with the world. The night before we went to eat at a Tex-Mex restaurant. As we sat down, the feelings of belonging revisited me just as they had when I was in Riviera Maya. As I discussed this with her, I could feel in my soul that Texas is where I was supposed to go instead of Oklahoma. I had never even considered visiting Texas, let alone moving there. Somehow, I knew that was my destination and now I had to figure out how to do that.

Several weeks after the conference, I decided to take on the challenge of walking on fire with my friends, another step to get rid of my fears. As crazy and daring as it sounds, it wasn't too difficult. So many things are stamped in our brains since childhood, like fears, control our limitations and future, but we can overcome them and change it all. If you have faith, you can achieve anything you want.

At the end of October, on a Monday morning, I called someone who had been in the USA many times; I told him about my plan, and he gave me the number of a girl from Quebec who was already in the USA. I contacted that person, and she told me that she had a place for me to stay. The place was Mission Ranch which was owned by the first American lady who trusted me to work on her horse and who suggested that I go to the BFA. And guess what! The ranch was in Texas. These were more than enough signs for me to know that was where I was meant to go.

Before the end of the day, I had found someone was also making the trip and whom I could follow. I had made all the appointments necessary to make sure my truck and trailer were ready to go and took care of everything for my "tech-teaching business" to keep going while I was gone. We left a few days later on Friday. The fact that everything had fit perfectly together showed that God had it all planned, and it was meant to happen.

Overflowing with excitement, I set out on my new adventure with my trusty little dog, Molly, to Texas. Molly was a trooper throughout the three days we spent on the road. I was also very lucky to have friends who like to talk on the phone, as that's what I did most of the time to keep me from being too bored or tired. It made time go by a lot quicker. When I reached my destination, I was very tired and, at the same time, way too excited to sit down (again!). I was proud of myself for this massive achievement of driving to Texas. I met some amazing people and even more awesome horses. Even though some days I only stayed in my trailer and worked, I was grateful to be in this new area and finally living my dream. Little did I know that I would be living in this tiny space for nearly two years!

What was even more amazing about this trip to Texas was that I was still only a few hours from Oklahoma City and still got to attend the BFA in December. It was my first time going to such a big barrel race. It was amazing to see and meet so many amazing equine and human athletes. The best part was to finally put some faces on the many people I had talked with over the phone and to get to touch and see all the horses I talked with. I absolutely loved the connection that I felt there.

Initially, I thought about driving back home for Christmas but eventually decided to fly there, then come back, and work on more horses. Deep down, I felt that it was the right thing to do.

Just before leaving, a well-known trainer asked me to visit her to communicate with her horses, since I didn't have the time to do so at the BFA. There was something in her and her horses' energy that blew me away, made me feel like she was an answer from God to all my questions. Of course, she didn't realize it then, and neither did I, but meeting her changed my entire life.

Chapter 5

Second trip

On January 6th, 2019, my daughter and I flew back together to Texas and from there, she went back to Oklahoma. On the way, she asked me about my plans because everyone else at the ranch had already moved to Edna, TX, for the futurity. 'I have no clue, honestly,' I told her. Before leaving, I had asked God to guide me on what to do. And as soon as I landed in Dallas, I received a message from the trainer I met before Christmas, asking me if I could come to Edna to talk to her horses. This was exactly the sign I was looking for! Without a hint of hesitation, I told her that I would be there the next day.

Traveling to Edna the next day was stressful! I didn't know where I was going, and I had to maneuver my truck and trailer through rush hour Dallas-Fort Worth traffic. Probably the most stressful drive of my life. I broke down in tears a few times and stayed on the phone with my mom almost the whole way for support, but I was so proud that I did it. I got there, parked my trailer, and got set up. I was, admittedly, scared and so much out of my comfort zone that I really just wanted to stay in my trailer to work on the horses I already had lined up over the phone. BUT I didn't drive all this way to take the easy way out and listen to the doubts in my head. I asked for a sign to go there and received it, so now I had to take action. That's how you grow. It's all about faith. If you ask for a clear sign, guidance from God, and you get it... have faith and listen to it!! Don't let doubts get the best of you! If you don't do it, I promise you'll regret it.

The next day, I got to work on communicating with the horses I went there for. In no time, I was swamped by horse communication requests!

Before I was even done with them, I had a line-up of horses waiting for me. These were the best horses in the industry trained by the most competent trainers in the business. I talked

Second trip

to at least 20 horses every day. I spent all my time and energy on them.

After a few days, I was completely drained. To be honest, I didn't know much about the barrel racing industry in the USA. I worked with a lot of famous trainers, and I had no idea who they were or what they had won. I didn't care that much; I was just happy to get to work with and help so many great horses. Gaining these trainers' trust was just the cherry on top.

At the end of the last day, on January 12th, 2019, I was so tired that I sat on a hay bale and closed my eyes to relax and unwind. I got a couple calls and text messages from this one number, but I was so exhausted that I ignored them. I didn't have the energy for another one. My daughter called me to ask me how it was going, so I told her the situation. She asked me who had been calling me. Weirdly enough, I didn't have that name saved in my contacts, but her name still appeared over her number when she called. I still wasn't very good at pronouncing names, so I sent her a screenshot of the missed call.

'Brittany Pozzi!?!', She yelled over the phone, 'you better get off your butt and find the energy to go talk to that horse! No is not even an option!' By the way she said that I knew she was serious. At the same time, one of my friends came to see me. He had heard that Brittany was trying to reach me and told me the same thing. I better find the energy to go.

Second trip

And so, I did. I was happy that my daughter made me do it because it was Brittany's world champion horse, Duke! Working with him was amazing! I know, yes, yes, you're probably wondering what the champion said, and how he was. Even if I would love to share the details, I won't tell you because confidentiality is important to me. I am sure that you would also appreciate that privacy if this was about your horse! Sorry if I don't answer your curiosity for now but I may share some anonymous stories somewhere in the book. I found the answers to many while learning my way through life, and now I can provide you with the tools that helped me bloom into a better version of myself.

That week had a major impact on my life. I asked for a sign from God, and He gave it to me. I listened, even when I felt scared. I believed in the sign that I received. If I had listened to my head, I would have definitely stayed in my horse trailer and played it 'safe'. That's the difference between connecting with your soul and thinking with your head. Your head always shows you the safe way and tries to keep you small, in your comfort zone. Sometimes, you need to overcome your internal personal limits to really accomplish what you are meant to do.

I met someone else that weekend who plays an important part in my journey, Tasha Welsh. Due to lack of time, I didn't get to talk with her horses in Edna, but I went to her house the week after. As I pulled in her driveway, I felt so peaceful and comforted. It was the first time in a while that I felt like I was at home. And it was the start of a great friendship.

The next trip I made was to Kinder, Louisiana. Taking my truck, trailer, and dog on the road was getting easier and easier. Once again, I got to work with many amazing athletes. Most importantly, that's where I met Dustin Angelle and Dr. Clay Espey. Dustin wanted me to talk to some of his horses, and as I started, I could see that Clay was very hesitant about it. What I didn't find out until later was that Clay is a vet. Good thing he wasn't the first one who would stand there with a concerned look and his arms crossed, I had learned to stay confident and not listen to those judgements. As I worked with those horses, I asked/told them about a certain injection, a certain time ago. Dustin told me that, no, they didn't do that. Made me sweat a little. But then, Clay looked at his notes and said that I was actually right, he did inject that horse where and when I said. Even though I wasn't doubting what the horse was telling me, I was finally able to take a deep breath and relax a little bit more. Clay's look also changed from suspicion to curiosity. Since then, I have visited them at their house multiple times, and we have built an amazing relationship. We really like to work together, and I have learned so much from both of them. As soon as I have a question about a horse, I know I can call Clay and he will share his knowledge with me and help me figure out the problem. And he does the same with me.

On my way back from Kinder, I received a text message from Tasha's vet, requesting me to visit a few horses with her. I was delighted, to say the least, and immediately accepted her invitation. I called Tasha to thank her and asked if the offer to park at her place was still available. Turns out she was more than

Second trip

happy to have me over. I went there a week later and met the vet the day after to look at some cutting horses, whom I had never talked to before. I was mind-blown and impressed by the horses; the way they moved, talked, and worked. I can even say that I fell in love with them.

Up to this point, I had only talked to horses, dogs, and maybe a few cats, but one day, I got asked to go talk to some bucking bulls! It was crazy, and so different, I enjoyed every second of it. They would show me how they like to buck, what makes them happy, what they don't like and what pain they might have. There was even one that was really mad at me, I didn't understand why. He explained to me that usually his owner goes in his pen and scratches him, but because I was there, he was standing outside with me. I told the owner about it, he laughed, walked in his pen,

and started scratching him. I always say that I put no doubt in the message I receive, but this one was so uncommon, it really surprised me.

I am grateful for all the experiences that God put on my journey since I learned how to put myself first, and I'm proud of who I am, without a doubt. I am glad that I have no fear of what others think of me. I know there are still people who judge my work and my abilities, and, you know, I can make mistakes too sometimes. But I always give my best to every animal that I talk to. Every day, I am thankful that God gives me opportunities to do good things in my life.

Second trip

I spent the rest of the winter traveling to various events with Tasha. We were at the Patriot in Fort Worth when I saw the Barrel Horse News. I told her that one of my biggest goals was to, one day, have someone talk about my work and how I helped them in this magazine. I took a copy and put it on the side of my fridge in my trailer. Every time I would look at it, I would thank God for the article, and I would visualize opening it and seeing my name in it. I didn't know when or how it would happen, but I wasn't worried about it, just really thankful.

In the middle of March, I was so excited when I found out that a couple of my friends from Quebec were coming to visit me. I was ecstatic because it had been a long time since I had French speaking people around me, and they brought me so much joy! As soon as they arrived, I received a message. Someone was in Stephenville and wanted me to help her mare. I didn't know her at all so I asked Tasha if the girl could bring her horse to her place instead of me going there. I also told her that I didn't really want to work right now because I wanted to spend time with my friends. I showed her the text message, she looked at me with excitement and told me I needed to go right away. Turns out, it was JLo, Ivy Seabens' prime rodeo horse. Hence, I went and was glad that I did. I was amazed by the communication. Since that day, I have been helping JLo and I enjoy working with her every time.

A few weeks later, my daughter graduated from College in Oklahoma, and I went there for her graduation ceremony. It was amazing to be able to be there for her, all while working long-distance. Such a great feeling to be able to do it all. To celebrate this success, my parents, one of my brothers and his family came all the way from Quebec for her special day. I made some great memories with her and our family. My parents helped me drive back to Canada after graduation. We stopped at the futurity in Fort Smith. I proudly presented my parents to my new friends and customers. I loved to get to show them my work, the difference I can make here and also the difference between barrel horses in Quebec and the USA.

Second trip

My mom, like many others at that time, could not understand how I was able to live in a such a small space. But for me, there was no doubt that it was a sacrifice that I needed to do to achieve my goals. Looking back now, I really don't know how I made it for so long in my 10x7 trailer, but it was all worth it.

I chose to stay in Quebec all summer, going to various events and continuing working on horses over the phone. However, I was missing my life in Texas. Somehow, I had left my heart there in the little time that I had spent in the States. I decided to go back in October 2019, to continue my work there, meet new people and horses, and attend more events. I was always on the road for futurities, and I stayed in my small trailer, enjoying the opportunities God put in front of me. I met a lot of great people on the road. I started working more on the vets, trainers, and equine chiropractors.

In December, I got invited to go to Las Vegas like I had manifested the year before! Some of my amazing customers asked me to go with them while their kids competed in the Junior NFR! I was so excited to go back! I knew I would get to go back because of my work, but never thought it would be from the communications! On top of it, I was also working with an amazing horse who

Second trip

qualified for the NFR, and her amazing owners got me tickets to go watch the rodeo with them! It was a great experience and a trip I will never forget.

As I've mentioned many times before, I always asked myself questions on what more or what else I can do to be my best self, to be on the right path and help others. One day, I had an idea to create an online clinic in English, just like I did with Vision Cheval. I decided to ask a trainer, one I had already worked with. Before I talked to her about this, I asked God for a sign. I said to God that if she's in, I would go forward with this idea. She replied in affirmative and reciprocated my energy regarding the idea. I was so excited about it! That gave me the energy to start. Even if her mind changed during the process, that was the answer, the sign that I needed that day to move ahead with this. Hence, Horse Konfidence was founded in March 2020. I was optimistic that with my knowledge and experience I would be able to help thousands of people. For me, it was a way to put my teaching skills and my animal communication together. Many famous people have been a part of my amazing journey, such as Brandon Cullins, Ivy Saebens, Troy Crumrine, Tasha Welsh, Billie Jack Saebens, Ryann Pedone, Dr. Shawna Turner, Dustin Angelle, Seth and Ashley Schafer, Pete Oen, and Kelsie Domer. And now it was time to make others' dreams come true.

I kept traveling to different states, going to various events to help more horses. I even had the chance to stay for a few months in Louisiana with Dustin Angel and Clay Espy. I really enjoyed my time with them. And most of all, I learned so much. Clay is a vet and Dustin, an amazing barrel horse trainer. They were both open-minded to work with me because we have the same goal, which is to make horses happy and healthy.

Since moving to Texas, I have already worked on thousands of horses. I was blown away by this success. My goal has always been to help the horses to the best of my capabilities. I wanted to innovate and find more ways where I could help not only the horse but also its rider to be their best. If you've ever worked with me, you've probably heard me say many times 'I'm not a psychic', I'm a translator. If I were a psychic, I'd buy the horses I knew would win it all, and I would bid my money on the winning racehorse. But I'm not, so I don't do that. I like to take the time to ask God things like "How can I help this specific horse more?", "How could I help all horses and their riders more?" or "How can I use my gift and let it shine even more?". That's when the idea of my VIP program came to mind. I realized I could only help so many horses through direct communication, and there's only so much I can do for them. And that's a limitation I didn't like to have! Of course, I can't talk with all the horses in the world, but the more horses I help, the better the chances for these and more horses over time to have a better quality of life. So, what if through this program I could educate and help people to get in tune with their horses' needs, connect with themselves, and achieve their goals. I want people to be able to understand their horses better and be a better team with them. This way, I could help a lot of people, and through them be able to help an insane number of horses.

While I started working on this program, I got to check something I had wanted to do for a while off my bucket list.

Second trip

Visiting Arizona. One of my very good friends asked me if I wanted to go on a three-day retreat in Sedona, not knowing it was even a goal of mine. Sedona is one of the most magical places to feel Earth's energy. I got to have a session with a Shaman who helped me to feel even more connected and confident. It was liberating, helped me destroy some limitations I had about saying out loud to the whole world that I was an animal communicator. This meeting and a whole lot of laughter with my friend made the whole trip magical.

On the last day of the trip, I received a phone call. I was invited to go to The Gauge Podcast. WOW! I said yes right away! Perhaps God sent me on this trip to find the confidence to say yes to this opportunity.

Nevertheless, I was terrified on the day of the interview. I almost turned back three times! What if people laughed at me? My

English is far from perfect, what if they didn't understand me? What if I say something wrong? And for the millionth time, I asked myself some questions. What is your goal? Will this be a step towards achieving it? I decided it would be a fun experience and if I only helped one person, then it's one more. Worst case scenario, I wouldn't have fun or wouldn't help anyone, but it wouldn't kill me. So, with a new perspective, I walked in and did it. Turned out, I had a lot of fun! They made me feel welcomed and comfortable. We talked a lot about communications, and I got to talk about my new VIP program. It was a hit and many people enrolled in my program, and I was so thankful for it.

In May 2021, I received a call from Barrel Horse News, they wanted to write an article about me. I had planted the seed for my name to be mentioned in the magazine without trying to control the when, how, or where. And instead, I got a four-page article written about me!! I can't ever thank God enough. That's the power of planting the seed and being grateful! Amazing things will happen!

This is why I am writing this book.

I wanted to share with you all the choices I had to make to put myself first and create the life I really wanted. During covid, I had to make many sacrifices and complex decisions in order to have my USA Visa, and I had to prioritize myself over my family. It was not always easy. But what comes out of it in the end is everyone being happy for me, and myself being very proud and happy about my progress and my life in general. I'm looking forward to a cool future.

I had to stay connected with my soul to keep aligned with my life path and purpose and make hard decisions along the way by prioritizing myself over my family needs. I was still present for them, at a distance, but it was not always easy! And I was really touched that they understood my decisions and supported me throughout the process.

I hope that the lessons I have learned from my life experiences and horse communications can be passed on to you so that you may be able to connect with and enjoy your horses more. Anything and everything is possible when you know how to ask, listen, and take action with the right tools for yourself and your animals so that you can achieve more success, and have a better quality life. Let's dive into the 10 most essential lessons that horses taught me!

PART 2

Life's tools

Train yourself, like you train horses

Our tack rooms often act as our treasure storehouses. Full of bits, headstalls, cinches, saddles, supplements and more, our tack rooms are where we go when we need to problem-solve. The horse is shaking its head? Maybe we need to try a different bit. It's having trouble rounding up? Use another saddle and see if it fits better. Our tack rooms are where we go in search of answers.

Since I related to animals a lot, I have found that certain principles in life are similar to the tools we keep in the tack room. Just like good horsemanship never goes out of style, neither do these tools. In the following chapters, we'll be discussing some of the tools that I have acquired over the years, and how they can be beneficial to us and our horses. For the purpose of making these tools as easy to understand as possible, I mostly use barrel horses in my examples. BUT this does not apply just to barrel horses, performance horses, or even only to horses. I use these same tools to help athletes and their horses in all kinds of disciplines. We always talk about horses being the athletes, but lately I've had the chance to work with some amazing human athletes, rough stock riders. It's been a great experience to work with them, figure out how to apply these tools to help them, show them a different perspective and also figure out how bucking horses and bulls think and work. All of these equine, bovine, and human athletes take it to a next level of intensity, and I really hope I can keep helping more competitors, so this book is for you too! I really wanted to create this book for anybody who wants to achieve their goals, be a better version of themselves, destroy their fears and old habits and much more.

The purpose of the previous part of the book was to share a part of my life with you so that you know about my experiences, the struggles I had growing up, discovering myself, and the growth and courage I found to take myself to the next step.

For as long as I can remember, I have always asked questions. Sometimes they are directed to God or the Universe, and sometimes I ask questions to myself, hoping to get the answers that can help open more possibilities, make more conscious decisions, and lead me toward my goals. I am always experimenting and exploring. Hence, I indulged myself in numerous books, trying to gain different perspectives. I also work with several mentors so that I can continuously expand my mind. I don't have all the answers to my questions, but I know that I won't stop looking for them. I continue to learn new things every single day, it's a daily routine, and this has helped me find some tools which have been helpful throughout my life and helped me connect more easily with the animals. All the tools are equally important to me, however, for the sake of this book, I categorized them. If you want, you can play around with these, ask yourself what you want and need, and dive into the exercises! Enjoy!

Chapter 6

Tool #1

What are your goals?

If goal setting (and achieving them) was a tangible object, a piece of equipment in your tack room, it would be your headstall and bit, because, just like your goals, they control the direction of your life. If our life feels adrift and purposeless, it is a good indicator that we are lacking goals and direction. Part of good communication with your horse is sending clear signals through your hands to the horse's head using the bit. Clearly defined goals serve the same purpose. They help set the direction of everything in our lives. If we don't have plans, we live in an unconscious routine, unaware of our life and our personal power.

Starting on this journey is simple. You only have to ask yourself what your goals are. What is success to you? Is it good health? Do you want a successful business? Is your goal to help others? Do you wish to feel more connected to your horses? Is it to be a good parent? Trainer? Spouse? A better friend? Feel more joy? Be more peaceful? Have more money? Feel free? Win a lot of races with your horse? There is no definite good or bad answer. You only need time to figure out what you really want. It's possible that what you desire today might not be what you want tomorrow. However, with consistency, you can figure out your heart's inner desires and set your goals accordingly. Find something that you love to do, something which you're passionate about, not something which will please other people around you, because you will never be truly happy with that. Just be honest with yourself, with no limits, as if everything is possible, and write it down.

If you have ever written your dreams and your goals before, make sure to read them again and see if they're still aligned with what you desire for your life. If not, you can erase them and add new ones. Try to be as specific as you can while writing down your goals, but don't get hung up on making them perfect. The important part is to write them down. You can always keep adding more or adjust it the next day. Take your time and feel comfortable with them. You need to ask yourself why you want a particular thing and how you want to become this person. If the reason makes you feel at ease, then, go for it.

What are your goals?

This is my first tool because with clear goals, making important decisions becomes easier when you know where you're heading. Essentially, clarifying your goals helps your entire life come into focus. When you have a list of goals, categorize them into short-term and long-term goals. The point of having a briefly written list of goals gives you a clear mindset of where you are heading. Everything after that is about choices and actions. Are we making decisions that take us closer to our goals or farther away from them? The clearer your goals are, the more you will become aware of your choices of what happens in your life.

Taking responsibility for your actions is a major part of achieving your goal. When you realize and accept that whatever happens in your life, good or bad, is because of your actions and decisions, you can take control of your life. You need to remind yourself that if you want something good to happen, you will have to take charge and make it happen. No one else is going to do that for you. Even if you were unaware of this simple thing, the moment you realize your own authority over your life, you are one step closer to achieving your dreams.

When bad things happen, you have to change your mindset from "why did this happen to me" and all emotions that come with it to "What can I do to change it? What can I learn from it?" "What's right about it I'm not getting?" Per example, very often people will blame the way they were raised for their misbehavior as adults. Even though your parents might not have raised you the best way possible, they did the best they could with the tools and consciousness they had at that moment. Now, you have the choice to accept it, learn from it and make other choices that will bring you where you want. Putting the blame on them is only going to make you take a few steps backwards. Your goal here should be to make the best of what you have around you, learn new tools, and become a better version of yourself.

The same goes for being a better rider. If you wish to be a better rider, and you watch numerous riding videos all day, but never practice it on your horse, then you are straying farther away from your goal. This circles back to personal responsibility; what's occurring in our lives is because of our choices. So, if you don't like the results you are getting, it's time to re-evaluate and make different choices. There is no room for victimization or self-pity when setting and achieving goals. If the current situation isn't working, it's because of our choices, and changing the path will get you a different outcome.

There is no good or bad decision if we learn from them. Learn from it and choose differently next time if you're not happy with the results, it's just an experiment. You can't change anyone's life, and no one can change yours. The only thing you can do is change yourself. If you have your goals and make good choices, you will get closer to your destination. If you have no plans and just go work and live for the weekend, that's okay too. That's your choice. Just know that you've chosen that yourself, and you are living for the days off.

It's your own choice to identify the goals that are more important to you and work to achieve them. Be intentional and think through what your most important goals are. Then make decisions that will propel you towards your goals. In other words, choose the right bit from your tack room to steer you clearly towards your purpose.

Chapter 7

Tool #2

Ask, listen

Sometimes we tend to ignore things we shouldn't. Sometimes the signs are clear, trying to speak to us, tell us something important, but due to many reasons - intentional or unintentional - we ignore them. Sometimes we are stuck somewhere, desperately looking for an answer, but we forget to do the most basic thing: ask for an answer and listen to it.

Simply put, the ask and listen tool is like the reins on the headstall. When you pull on your reins, you are expecting an answer from your horse. And what's important is that to get the desired action or result, you need to ask first. I apply this tactic in my life as well. Whenever I have a question, I just ask the Universe and/or God about it. I ask for a clear sign, then I listen. Intently. That is the most important part. So many times, we ask, but don't listen to the signs. We underestimate listening to what many call our intuition. This is one thing which can answer all your questions without frantically looking from one place to another. The more I use the *Ask, listen* tool, the easier I find it to be set on the right path.

So, how can we apply this tool in our lives and master it? It's simple. Practice makes it easier over time, right? So, you keep practicing. It's easy to ask questions, but what takes time is keeping your ears, mind, and soul open and listening. When I am working with people in my Rider's Konfidence VIP program, I urge them to start by asking and listening to their bodies and their needs. Do I need to eat right now? What should I eat? Is a nap what I need at the moment? Should I go to sleep earlier today? Do I need to exercise? Ask your body these questions, take a few moments and listen to what it says. The answer can be in any form; it could be an image in your mind, an idea, or an emotion. Make sure to follow what your soul feels without doubting it. Your body is telling you exactly what it needs, and you must do exactly what it tells you to do. For example, if you ask your body what it wants for breakfast, wait and listen. If you suddenly feel a craving for some juicy steak, then go ahead and have steak! Don't overthink that having steak is not the brightest idea for breakfast. If your body wants it, then have it! And if you feel full after just three bites, ask your body if it needs to eat more, wait for the answer, and just eat more if you want to. You don't have to force yourself to eat it all if you don't want to. What you need to do is break away from the norms imposed by society. It's that simple! The point is that you start practicing with your daily simple tasks so that you'll become able to listen to more complicated ones.

When you are about to make a decision, a major one, you need to ask God certain questions. The power of questions opens numerous possibilities. What can I do to change my situation? How can I bring more joy to my life? Would this particular choice make me feel good about myself? Does that choice empower me or enslave me? Will this choice bring me closer to my goal or farther? Am I choosing for myself or to please others?

Now, you need to be very mindful while looking for the answers, since it may take any form, it chooses to. Perhaps you're just conversing with your best friend, and they casually mention something, but it strikes a chord and makes you realize what you've wanted all along. It could be in the form of a dance, a song, an image, or a feeling. Just remember that no matter what the answer is, you have to act according to it. Action will bring you closer to your answer and will make you feel light and more connected to yourself.

I try to apply this tool whenever I feel stuck or torn in between choices, and it always helps me to clear my thoughts by asking the right questions, being patient, and listening for the right answer.

So, you're probably thinking, how do I look out for these answers? Here is how I do it. I become aware of my surroundings and actively keep my eyes and ears open to see and hear the signs. Sometimes I get a feeling that guides me toward the right path. I also ask myself 'Does it make me feel light or heavy?' Most likely, what feels lighter for you is the right answer. This allows me to assess the situation for myself. If I realize that it's heavy but necessary, then I like to play around with the question by asking 'How can I make this lighter for myself?' And sometimes, just asking these questions makes me feel at ease.

One of the big goals with this is to be able to ask and listen with your horse. What does my horse need right now? What is he trying to tell me? Does he need to be fed? How can I help him grow? How can I grow with him? However, it's important that you keep using this tool on yourself to be effective on your horse as well. The more you focus on your awareness of yourself, the more you will be aware of your horse at the same time.

I was working with some friends and their horses, and I asked them to try this tool. At first, they were skeptical about it, but they tried it. They called me back about a week later and told me how amazed they were with the results. They intently listened to what the horse had to say and implemented it. They really noticed when he was happy about something and when he wasn't. It had completely changed their connection with their horse for the better, and he had better performance too!

One very important factor which can help you in your communication with your horse is energy. You need to make sure that you're giving your best positive vibe around your horse. Before starting any communication with any horses, I always ask myself, 'What kind of energy do I need to hold, so I can be the best for this horse?' Then I take a deep breath before I initiate the conversation. In case I feel that I might not be my best self at the moment for this specific horse, I wait for the appropriate time because each animal deserves the best version of me, so I can help them to the best of my abilities.

Don't forget to apply this tool to your relationship with your horses. When talking to your horse, ask them whatever question you want and trust them. Ask them how you can be a better rider for them, or how you can have better runs together while having more fun. Then wait for the horse to answer you. Look for what you feel inside and follow it. I asked one of the trainers to attempt this. She asked two of her horses what they needed. For one, she instantly felt confidence and quietness, while for the other, she felt that the horse needed joy and her presence. She applied these qualities in her runs, allowing the horses to perform to the best of their abilities. Another trainer also experimented with this with his 4-year-old barrel horse in a huge race. The horse had issues in his first barrel. But then he trusted his instincts and decided to let the horse run to the first barrel like an open (more experienced) horse instead of schooling him further. To his awe, that was one of the most perfect first barrels he had ever turned!

The horses understand these questions much better than we think they do. They may answer you in various ways depending on what is required. Some might respond with 'Let me do my job', while others may say 'Be quiet, and listen to what I tell you daily.' Our horses are telling us what to do and how to help them every day. They feel your energy, speak through their souls, and provide you with a solution based on that. What you have to do is carefully listen to them, and without doubting what you've heard, act on it so that you can be the ultimate help they need.

If someone had told me four years ago that my life would be the way it is right now, I would have laughed at them in disbelief, because never would I have imagined it to be this amazing. My life has shifted since I started asking and listening. I feel more connected, happier, and complete now. I would urge everyone reading this book to try this because you all deserve joy, lightness, and ease in your life! When you build a regular habit of using this method, don't be afraid to ask for bigger and better things. Everything you desire is there for you, you simply need to ask God, the Universe, and your soul, then listen to the answer.

When you make a habit of practicing to ask and listen, you will take your life by the reins and maneuver it yourself to the direction you desire, instead of living this life according to other people's plans for you. You will become more responsible as you will be actively making intentional decisions for critical matters. It helps to be aware of the possibilities and make the right choices, to achieve your goals. You will feel more grateful because you will be aware of all the blessings that the Universe and God have bestowed on you. This tool is the perfect way to start taking responsibility for your life and build a better relationship with yourself and your animals.

Chapter 8

Tool #3

Make a choice and take action

With each tool, we take it a step further, a step towards achieving your goals. The make a choice and take action tool is comparable to your saddle. Most horses can feel every move you make in the saddle. People often don't realize this, but a lot of horses I have talked with put a big focus on the way they feel their rider moves in the saddle.

Sometimes you might be giving the horse the right cues, but the saddle doesn't fit correctly, so the end movement is not the right one. It's the same thing with life; you might be making the right choice, but there is something blocking you from the end result you are expecting. A change is needed. Something between the choice and the action has to change.

However, sometimes you are simply not giving the right cue. You cannot expect your horse to slow down for a turn if you are in the front of the saddle. You cannot expect your horse to run faster if you are sitting back in your saddle. You cannot move your hips to the left and expect your horse to make a nice, balanced turn to the right. Once again, it's the same thing in your life. You cannot make the same bad choices over and over again and expect the outcome to be different. If you want to achieve your goals, you need to take actions and make choices that will take you in the exact direction you desire. And sometimes, your horse will need you to be calm and as still as possible in your saddle to let him work.

I'm sure you have guessed it by now, it's the same in your life: if you keep trying new things, making new choices, and nothing is working, take a moment to be still, ask new questions, and let God speak to you and guide you through the proper actions. Take a step back and let him take the reins, and enjoy the ride, not everything has to be done at 100mph! Taking the time to make a clear plan about what you want out of life will align you to the correct actions to take.

Make a choice and take action

You are making choices every day, every hour, and every second of your life. Some are big, some are small, it doesn't matter. Whether you choose to relax, eat, work, ride your horse, do the laundry, read a book, etc., the choice is yours and yours only.

I often hear people say, 'I didn't have a choice'. This is something that I do not believe in. We always have a choice. It might not be an easy one, some choices are hard to make, but you still get to decide. The question here is, do you choose for yourself or to please others? Whichever choice you make, there are no good or bad ones, it all depends on the reasoning behind it (as long as this decision aligns with your moral compass and values). So, we've already taken the time to write our goals and priorities. Now, when it comes to making a decision, just ask yourself: does this choice bring me closer to or farther from my goals? Make a choice and take action. Don't doubt it, don't think about it for a while, take the next step and move forward. Even if it is a tiny step, anything that gets you closer to your own goals is worth it. It is not always going to be easy; you'll need to put in the effort, but in the end, you'll be glad you did. It's all going to be worth it.

I am a huge believer in the fact that we are responsible for what happens in our life. Adversity can hit anyone at any time. However, the outcome all depends on how you handle it. If you are not comfortable with a situation, you need to ask yourself, "how can I change this?" Think of what decisions you can make to change your circumstances. If the situation you are in is because of a previous decision that did not bring the expected result, ask yourself, "what can I learn from this?" and "what do I need to do differently this time?" It's the same way with your horses. When you move in the saddle, pay attention to the way your horse reacts. Does he go too fast, move his hips or shoulders too much? Every action that you take brings a result. The more you are aware of it, the more you can connect with your horse and change the movement and action that will help you both as a team. Take the time to feel his movement and move with him.

Make sure not to dwell in the 'victim' mode. What I mean is, do not overthink when you get stuck in a wretched situation and go 'Why did this happen to me?' This is harmful to your mental health and can deviate you from your goal. At the start of the book, I shared a few personal stories. My purpose wasn't to be pitied and make you say 'Oh, what a sad story.' In fact, I intended to tell my story the way it was, how difficult my childhood was at times, and that I was literally struggling with life to show you that I never gave up on myself and kept working to get better. I am grateful for all the experiences that I have had, even when they were unfortunate or uncomfortable, because they made me who I am today. And I'm proud of coming out as a better and stronger version of myself. I am still very far from perfect, and I still have a lot more to learn. Being perfect is not my goal. I strive to be "perfectly imperfect" ! I must add, it is absolutely ok to have bad days, and sometimes need to take a break. You don't have to fix everything right there and now. Some days are just rough days. Accept it and move on as soon as you're ready.

I have said many times already that I like to be connected to myself as much as I can, and I try to find new ways to do it. Sometimes it helps me figure out which choice to make, but

Make a choice and take action

sometimes it doesn't. Which is why it's also very important to ask different questions and to have outside sources helping you. I like to read new books, listen to new podcasts or documentaries, ask friends and/or have sessions with a mentor to have a new perspective on things. Not every choice will be easy and quick to make, so having various kinds of outside resources can be helpful. You can learn from their experience and knowledge. Furthermore, it is important to know when you have outgrown a certain method, and it is totally acceptable to change the way you do things and get a new mentor or coach. Always have something or someone in your corner that will get you out of your comfort zone, that will keep lighting that spark in you. Sometimes it's just a movie that I am watching or a random conversation with someone which will ignite the fire inside me and tell me 'It's time to change, Katheleen.' This is when I know that my time to make new decisions has arrived. Once again, same thing in the saddle. Maybe after a while, your riding style has changed so much that your saddle doesn't fit your needs anymore. Or your horse's muscle mass has changed, and it doesn't fit him well anymore. You won't keep riding that saddle, you'll try another one or at least look at different options. Why don't you do the same with yourself? Don't forget, you always have the choice.

Currently, one of my major goals is to feel more joy. Hence, every morning when I wake up, I ask myself 'What kind of energy can I create to feel more joy?' Or simply, 'How can I feel more joy today?' Those who know me well, know that I need a good cup of coffee first thing in the morning. So, to enhance my joy, I have a good espresso machine. Every morning, I prepare an aromatic cup of coffee - the process itself is therapeutic to me - and I enjoy every sip I take. For me, this is one of the best ways to give joy to myself at the beginning of the day. What works for me doesn't mean it will work for you. Thus, you need to find your own goals and own ways to feel joy. It's the same with horses too. What works with one horse might not work with another, so pay attention to them and learn what they like, so you can embody the best energy for that horse.

I am not trying to give you all the answers here. I am just trying to give you as many tools as possible, so you can make your own choices as confidently as possible. Keep in mind that you and only YOU are responsible for your actions and your life. The more conscious you are about your decisions, the more control you will have over your life. We all deserve a life full of happiness and joy, and we must make the decisions that will get us closer to happiness.

Chapter 9

Tool #4

Destroy your fears

The tool 'destroy your fears' is like the pitchfork and wheelbarrow in your barn because this will help you clear the shit out of your life. The thing about a pitchfork and wheelbarrow is that they only serve a purpose when they are put to work consistently. If you just let them lean against the barn wall, all the horse manure will keep piling up all over the stall, until the space becomes unlivable. Your fears are like that, too. If you keep letting them pile up in your mind and let them take over your life, your life will be filled up with shit and the stink will keep every good thing away. It will stop you from achieving your goals and be a limitation in your mind.

What keeps you from going forward? Is it your fears? A limitation? Something that was instilled in you as a child? I have had a lot of fears and limitations in my life, and still get them all the time. Fear doesn't go away; you learn to destroy it more easily over time. There are many tools that have helped me get through these tough times. They have made it a lot easier for me to destroy fears quickly when they arise.

The first step toward destroying fears is asking yourself questions regarding them. It is easy to know when you're afraid of something, but the hard part, and what is needed to be able to destroy them, is to figure out the root of the fear. Where does it come from? For example, I used to be very afraid of people's judgments. Because of this, I made a lot of choices only to please people. It kept me from doing a lot of things I wanted to do, and, even, from being myself. Now, when I'm afraid of doing something, I ask myself: What is blocking me from doing it? Then, let's say that it's because I don't want to be judged by others, I turn that into a question. What's the worst that can happen if they judge me? It's most likely not going to kill me. I might feel uncomfortable, but, oh well, that feeling won't last.

The pride from overcoming a fear and doing something that makes you happy will overpower any negative emotions. Plus, it's their own problem if they judge you. Ask yourself why you wanted to do it in the first place. Most of the time it's something that your soul needs, something that will make you happy or something that will help others. As I already shared with you, I was very afraid of going on The Gauge podcast. I was afraid of people's judgment, what they would think of my work, the way I speak in English, or if I said something wrong. When I realized my fear, I told myself that I had to destroy it. As simple as this may sound, what works best for me is to tell myself to 'destroy this fear' repeatedly until I feel the energy shift in me, and the fear loses its grip. After that, I realign with my goals. With the podcast, my goals were to have fun and be able to help at least one person. The worst-case scenario was that I wouldn't be of help to anyone, and I wouldn't have fun. Would that kill me? Of course not! I can give you many examples from my life where I have destroyed my fears and proceeded forwards. Asking questions and changing my goals is what has helped me go through and enjoy the experience.

I realized that other aspects that were blocking me from achieving my goals were the limitations that I absorbed when I was younger or the ones that came from society in general. I understood that it was taking a lot of space in my mind, and it's nobody's fault. Yes, my parents raised me and my brothers the best way possible. They taught us to take care of others, be there for each other, and to make the best decisions and choices for ourselves. And don't get me wrong, I'm very thankful for everything that they did for me. They raised me with the tools and the knowledge that they had at that moment in their lives, and I know that they did the best they possibly could. They still try their hardest for us every day, and I love them very much for it. Now, it is my job to take all their advice about work, finances, friendship, what I can do or not, what is good or bad for me, what I should or should not do, and make my own recipe from it. What I do with it can help me, or it could potentially hurt me. I have to use my own judgment and decide what is good for me, what works for me, and build my own life accordingly.

Let's go back to our horse shit example. If you take it and put it in your garden, it's going to help your plants grow. But if you just leave it in the stall where your horse spends most of his time walking around in it, breathing it, it can be very harmful to him. So, when I realize that there is a limitation programmed in my mind that keeps me in an unhealthy, shitty situation that's keeping me from moving forward, I erase it, so I can have the space to create a new, healthy one. The process is very easy. I just pretend to write the limitation in my mind, highlight it and then press "delete". It is really important to actually visualize it, it helps this process tremendously. Then, I replace this old programming in my mind with a new one, which is that I deserve everything and that it will come easily to me. I repeat it to myself until I feel comfortable with it and feel it deep down inside of me. I learned a mantra from Dr. Dain Heer that I have implemented in my life: 'All of life comes to me with ease, and joy, and glory.' As soon as I feel some fears coming up or something blocking me, I repeat this sentence until I feel better and more confident. Sometimes, I might say this at least 50 times a day!

You can either let your limitations and fears control you, or you can work on them and change the way you perceive them. You have this choice. Your horse also feels the same way. They can sense your fear or confidence and act according to that. Very

Destroy your fears

often, your horse's reactions depend on your emotions. So, if you are nervous before a race and your horse won't go in the alleyway, well guess what, your horse feels your fear and will most definitely not want to go in the alley because he's feeling your stress. If you are scared of the alley, then why would he ever want to go there? If you are so nervous about a bad performance, your horse will get very nervous too and his focus will not be about making a good performance. He will just focus on the nervousness and probably everything else around that could scare him. You cannot lie and hide your feelings from your horse or yourself. Destroy these limitations and fears you have created and be the confident person your horse needs you to be and who you need to be for yourself. You have the power to change your mindset and become the positive and confident person needed to achieve your goals. You just have to make the choice of doing so.

Chapter 10

Tool #5

Be present

This tool might be the most important one, but also the most difficult one to apply. To be present, it sounds pretty simple. This tool is like your cowboy boots, once you put them on, you know what you're about to do. Once you get in the saddle, you don't have to worry about your feet staying in the stirrups. You know your boots will keep you focused and in place. They give you the power to maneuver your horse better. Being in the present moment does the same thing, it keeps you focused, strong, stable, and gives you the power to set yourself up for success.

When you allow your mind to worry about the future, and anticipate what could happen or not, you feel more anxiety and stress. When you're dwelling in the past, you stay stuck in deception, and regrets, and often deal with the same situation all over again. Don't forget that you are a creator. You can create anything you can think of. Being in the present moment means connecting with yourself more, enjoying the moment to the fullest, living your life to the best, looking around in the present to seek answers to your questions, and achieving your goals, one at a time.

The most important place to apply this tool is when you are riding your horse. I have communicated with countless horses that tell me their rider is not with them when they ride. "She's riding me, but she's thinking about something else." or "Before going into the show pen, she just thinks that I won't do my job because of the last show." "He just thinks about the barrier that I have to go through." "She just thinks about the second barrel, and she changes her mind about how to ride me a million times." All your anticipation, stress, and anxiety, your horse feels it, and understands it. So, you transfer it to them.

Being in the present moment when riding your horse can help you to figure out a lot of things that you might not even think you can understand. Being fully focused on your horse can help you understand each other a lot better. You can feel if there is something wrong with him, even the smallest soreness or lameness. You can figure out if you are asking the right way, if your body is giving the right cue, if he can do it with less help, if he needs more help for certain movements, if he likes the

Be present

training, etc. If you are not completely focused on your horse, it is easy to miss small details, like the position of your body, and then it results in not understanding why your horse is not responding and doing the movement you were expecting. This tool of being present gives you the opportunity to enjoy and understand your horse better. It's actually very simple to practice, but our human minds have this habit of wanting to plan everything and complicate things. The more you will do this, the easier it will get, and you will actually find out how much more energized you can feel.

You need to intentionally stay focused on the present moment, especially at a competition. Before you get on your horse, or while warming up, you need to ask yourself about what kind of energy can you be at this time to be the best rider for your horse. Listen to yourself to hear the answer. I know it can sound weird, but your subconscious knows what you need to be, so the first thing you hear, or feel, listen to it, and do it. After this, ask your horse what kind of energy he can be to perform his best. Listen to what he says. This helps build an unbreakable bond with your horse because you're trusting him and telling him to trust you. We have talked about this with tool #2 Ask and Listen, and it is the same principle, it can be applied in many areas of your life.

It's the same with your life too. What do you feel in the present moment? What do you need? How are you? Being present in the moment gives you the chance to create more opportunities, destroy your fears as soon as you feel them, make the right choices for yourself, and create the life that you want and deserve. When you put your boots on, get ready to take life for a ride, let your worries out, concentrate on what you're doing right at this moment, and stop thinking about anything else that needs to be done.

Not only does being present in the moment helps you connect with yourself more deeply, but it also helps you save your energy. While doing the one task you are currently working on, if you also think about 10 other tasks, you are basically spending energy as if you were doing them, draining you way faster than you should be. When you are thinking about too many tasks at the same time, your brain doesn't register whether the task is being done at the moment or later. So, when you keep thinking about doing laundry the whole day, when you eventually do it at night, you'll be exhausted from it already, because you have already been doing it 10 times that day! Been there? I'm not laughing at you right now, I do it all the time too! But the more I practice being present, the easier it gets, the more energy I have, and the better I feel with myself.

You have to find what works for you to BE present in the moment. It's different for everyone. Many people practice meditation or yoga to stay mindful and focus on the present moment. I have an extremely fast brain, and I was always thinking too much, not able to stay focused while doing any of these exercises. I tried so hard to meditate, but I could only stay focused for 30 seconds, then my mind would go back to wandering about everything else. It ended up being more frustrating for me and would actually burn more of my energy because I was working so hard to try to stay focused. Then a friend of mine taught me an easy and effective trick to stay in the

Be present

present. He told me to start with the small things. For example, if I am washing the dishes, I should only think about washing the dishes. If I feel like my mind is losing focus, I look at the cup that I am washing and think 'I am washing this cup'. Then I continue this with the cutlery too, until I am done. You don't have to say it out loud, just keep your mind focused on doing what you are doing. That's living in the moment. It looks very simple and easy, but it was hard for me. Now, after a lot of practice, when I feel that my mind is going back to its old habit of overthinking, it's much easier to stop now.

Another way to do it, if you have kids around you, is to sit on the floor with them. Put your phone down and be present with them. Look at them play, interact with them, and see how they live the joy of the present moment.

So, when you brush, prepare, and ride your horse, just try to stay there mentally. It actually works! Don't just take my word... You need to try it and see it for yourself!

Chapter 11

Tool #6

Breathe and smile

Good forage and water is essential for your horse to survive. Adding supplements can help with their physical and mental health. There are supplements for everything: joints, hair, feet, etc. One very popular type of supplement helps with a horse's anxiety or stress. But did you know that the most important supplement they can rely on to solve that problem is actually YOU? And a great way to help your own anxiety and stress is through breathing and smiling. We obviously breathe without thinking about it every second of our life but adding mindful breathing exercises can help you in so many ways. Your horse feels you when you are either anxious or calm. Your horse can feel how fast your heart beats and when it changes speed. He can feel how fast or slow, deep or shallow you are breathing. So, if you get very nervous, your horse will feel it and many will get even more nervous than you. Some horses might read this nervousness as incoming danger, which is why they get stressed behind the arena. Even if you tell your friends that you are confident, and you got this, your horse feels what's deep inside of you. You can't lie to your horse.

There are many different breathing exercises available online, I know you can find one that fits you best. The one that I like to use the most is called the Wim Hof Method. This guy is able to control his body temperature with his breathing methods. It's incredible!

I created a breathing exercise for riders to use before a race to help them release stress and anticipation, be more confident, and be more connected to their horse. I tested this exercise with a few people, and they had great results with it! They felt a positive change in their mindset and saw a good change with their horses' performance, too. After they tested it out, I connected with their horses to see what they thought about it. That's the true test. People can lie to me about their feelings, but not to their horse. Initially, the horses are able to feel a big difference, but the most important part here is consistency over time. After just a couple of times of doing the exercise, horses were more relaxed and enjoyed the race more. However, when things started to go well, the riders tended to forget to maintain the practice. As a result, the horse's anxiety came back, and often

Breathe and smile

with more intensity. Breathing is free, simple, and doesn't take much of your time. It is an excellent tool to add to your warm-up that will help you and your horse tremendously.

This tool is not only important for your connection with your horse, it's great for the connection with yourself. It's something that can be practiced daily in your life. Whenever you are feeling sad, angry, anxious, or just in a bad mood, realize what you are feeling and try a breathing technique to make everything feel lighter. This clears your mind and helps you find the right answer to move forward. No one else can do it for you. It is your own responsibility, take the time to make yourself feel better.

Along with breathing, another very important and effective tool is smiling. It helps you feel amazing and radiates so many positive vibes. Have you ever been having a bad day, you go to the grocery store and, while minding your own business, someone smiles at you, and you smile back in common courtesy? Then, after a while, you realize that you feel much better. It's such a simple action that has so much power. I often do this when I go out. I smile at people who glance my way to see their reactions. Most of them smile back! When you smile at someone, you are helping them have a better day, and you never know who could really need it. It's free, it's uplifting for other people, and it's certainly good for you too. It's good for all the muscles in your face, and it can change your energy in a very positive way. When you are with your horse, smile and sing while riding so that they are able to feel the joy that you have with them too. It's so much fun! So, along with your morning breakfast, make it a habit to smile, it's the best supplement you can add to your life! You will feel an immense difference in your own personal attitude and your horse's performance. The rides will be so much more enjoyable. You will feel like you are ready to take on the day with full exuberance!

Chapter 12

Tool #7

Take care of yourself

It goes without saying; it's very important to take care of yourself to have a healthy life. As simple as this may sound, it is usually the last thing on our to-do list. Actually, do you even write anything about taking care of yourself on your daily to-do list? I know your horse has a whole list of specialists ready to take care of him at any time. I am sure your horse has a veterinarian, a farrier, a chiropractor, a massage therapist, an animal communicator, and probably more. You make sure that your horses have everything they need as soon as they need it, and you spend tons of money and time on them. What do you do for yourself? Do you take care of yourself? Not only does taking care of yourself has a huge impact on your whole life, but it can also be very beneficial for your riding. When your truck or horse trailer requires an oil change or simply to make sure that the tires are in condition to go on the road, you make sure to do what needs to be done. You wouldn't leave to go somewhere with a flat tire, or a broken tie rod. Similarly, your body is the vehicle that takes you on the road of life. You only have one. When picking a car, you make sure the ride will be smooth, safe, and enjoyable, right? Well, you have this body and mind for your whole life, so what are you doing to make sure it will be enjoyable and will be in the best shape for as long as possible? Do you have pain in your back, knee? Do you get headaches? Are you exhausted? Are you taking care of these issues? What are you doing for yourself? Or are you completing all the tasks that need to be done for your horses, house, barn, ignoring your own needs, and feeling mentally and physically drained by the end of the day?

When explaining the importance of this tool, I like to use the example of flying. As you board a plane, the first thing that the flight attendant talks about is that in case of an emergency, you need to put on your own oxygen mask before helping your kids or neighbors with theirs. This should be your all-time priority in life, too. If you are not taking care of yourself properly or getting proper rest, you will not be able to perform to the best of your abilities regarding any task. In addition, you won't be able to be your best self to help and support others if you don't help yourself first. You can't pour from an empty cup.

Take care of yourself

Even when riding, your horse is able to feel what is bothering you and if you are in pain. I've had many conversations with horses that have made me realize the importance of this connection and the frequency of issues stemming from a rider's pain. Some of these horses explained that they moved a certain way to keep the rider under them. Let me give you a few examples. A trainer that I work with had the same trouble with different horses. Talking with them, I found out they all said that the trainer put more pressure on one leg to compensate for the other. When I told the trainer about it, he said that he had pain in one of his knees, but he didn't have time to work on it. Since he had not worked on it and tried to fix it, this had created a problem for him and the horses. Not realizing that he was unbalanced in his saddle, he created different cues for the horses that changed their movements, either trying to understand the new position or trying to catch up with him. Addressing his knee pain was an easy fix that could've avoided a lot of problems. He just had to work on himself.

In another example, a horse went from having perfect barrels to not turning them tightly or as smoothly. The rider tried everything. She changed his routine, took the horse to the vet, and much more, but nothing worked. When she asked me to talk to him, the horse said that he felt like he had to work differently to keep his rider safe in the saddle. He said that she had some pain in one hip that kept her from riding as confidently as before. I found it slightly weird, but I knew I had no doubt in what he told me. So I called the owner and talked to her about it. She said that, yes, she had a problem with her hip. The horse really knew her well and did all he could to keep her safe. I am forever impressed by how good horses connect with their owner.

We are so focused on everything else, that we don't realize how much our own pain has an impact on everything around us. The more you are connected to yourself, the more you will feel everything your body needs. It might be harder at first because you will have a lot of work to do, and your body might ask for more because you are finally listening to it. The more you take care of it, the easier it will get, and your whole lifestyle will be more enjoyable. Everything you do for your horse; you should do for you. You train your horses, so they are in good shape and have the muscle memory to run. You should too. You think they would benefit from a certain supplement, so they get it. You should too. Their muscles feel tight, so they get a massage. You should too. They get the best food for their needs. You should too. You let them have a day off, so they can rest, recover, and relax. You should too!

A lot of people say, 'I should have done this earlier', which I don't like to hear. For some experiences in life, that's ok because that's how you learn. Not for your body. You only have one, and if you don't take care of your pains, they might be there permanently. You should talk to your body just like you would talk to a friend in need, and ask what it needs, wants, and prefers. Listen and make the choice to take care of it and do what is needed. You might not realize right now how much it can affect you, but after you take care of yourself, you'll realize how much easier everything else is, and you will get a lot more accomplished. It will help you achieve so many goals, your quality of life will be a million times better and everyone around you will also benefit from it.

Chapter 13

Tool #8

Take a step back

Every athlete likes to look at videos from their performance and analyze them. Looking at the good and the bad sets you up for the next competition. How many times have you looked at your videos over and over, watching every little detail, trying to find the small things that could have made you a tenth of a second faster or a point higher? How many times have you thought, before watching your run, that you rode your horse exactly how you should've, and it's your horse's fault that your run/ride wasn't perfect? Then, you watch the video and realize that you pulled a stride too early, you weren't positioned correctly, you weren't looking in the right spot... It is the same thing in our life. Sometimes we are too close to the problem and all we see is the perspective we have stuck in our head. And most of the time we think that everything around us is the problem, that we don't control our situation and there's nothing we can do about it. Just like the way we were thinking about the run before we watched our video. That's when the "Take a step back" tool comes in. Once you take a step back from what you felt during your run and take a look at the video from another perspective, you realize that there was something you actually could've changed to make it better. Let's do the same thing with any problems that occur in your life. When you can't seem to be able to move on or find a solution, take a step back and try to see the problem from another perspective. We feel stuck and lack creativity because we've been studying it from a micro-perspective for too long. Take a step back and look at the whole picture.

When you watch your videos, you take the time to analyze every detail. How the ground was, how you were sitting and moving in your saddle, how your timing was with your horse, how he was positioned around the barrels, if he looks comfortable or in pain, if the bit fits him well, and more. You take the time to look at every angle of your run before deciding what needs to change, and what works well. You need to implement the same analysis in your everyday problems. Sometimes we get tunnel-vision about our problem and can't seem to see a way out. You can ask, "What good is coming from this situation that I'm not seeing right now?" So take a step back, smile, breathe, relax, and start looking at every detail of the problem from different

Take a step back

perspectives. Sometimes when you look at the bigger picture, what seemed like a giant problem, may not even be one. Or the solution might be very simple. So take your time, let the solution come to you, listen to the answer, and voilà! The problem is solved. Let go of it!

The next step is to learn from the problem, find out what questions you asked yourself, what you understood from it, how differently you handled it and how you can learn from it for the next time you face adversity. It will get so much easier to solve problems each time because you will get better and quicker at realizing what is happening. Learning to take a step back will keep you from getting stuck, wasting time, creating a limited mindset and slowing down your growth. Look at the situation that you are in and imagine it was your best friend going through it. What would you suggest to him or her? What do you think (s)he needs to change or do to go through it positively?

The step back helps you to see different options and take out the negative emotion that you are stuck with. The goal is really not to be perfect. Anyway, what is perfect for me is probably not the same for you. And as a lifelong perfectionist, I like to say now that I'm perfect in my imperfections. We all make mistakes, and that's ok. Acknowledge when it happens, and then make a different choice next time. Is it really a mistake if you learn? This is a long-term, goal-achieving tool to help you create your dream life and connect to yourself and your animals in a whole new way. It will help you minimize problems instead of making them a big deal. Your days will be so much more enjoyable when your focus shifts away from the issues you face and onto the positive things in the present moment.

Looking at your performance videos helps you find the right solution to perform better with your horses and understand them better. Taking a step back in your life will help you find the right solutions with minimal friction and will help you understand and enjoy your life even more.

Chapter 14

Tool #9

Gratitude

Gratitude. That's all you have to remember from this chapter. It's the most important thing in life. Be grateful about everything. The good and the bad. God has created every detail of this life for you, and everything has a purpose. Even the bad days. They are there to make you grow, change your path and teach you something. So be always grateful. It's a staple in my daily routine. Like an old cowboy's cowboy hat, he never starts the day without it, wears it throughout the day until carefully hanging it up as he goes to bed. This is part of his routine every day. He may do it automatically, but he always treats his hat with due reverence. Being grateful should be the same way. Practice it daily, wear gratitude throughout the day from the moment you wake up to the moment you close your eyes.

Are you grateful for what you have in life? A supportive family, good friends, animals that devote their life to you, a great job, to be able to walk, and even to be able to get up in the morning and breathe. Material possessions are important, but they should be at the bottom of your list as they are temporary, replaceable things. Are you grateful for every beautiful thing life has given you? The more I am thankful to God for everything that I have, the more I feel God's and Universe's love and help around me. Just think how rewarding it is when you help someone, even if they haven't asked for your help, and they are very thankful, uplifted, and they express their appreciation for you. It makes you feel a lot of joy, and you feel thankful that you were able to help them too, right? The chances that you will want to help them again are pretty high. The happiness and the feeling of power it gives you is enough to make your whole day better, and you want to do it again and again. Let's look at the other side, though. You help someone with something pretty small, but they don't seem to care, be happy about it, or thank you for it. Even if it wasn't that big of a deal, does it make you want to help them again? No. So be thankful for all the help you get, and more help will come around. God and the Universe work in the same way. They have created your path and are there to help you. If you want them to help you even more, you have to notice everything they do for you, be happy and thankful about it. That's all God wants: your

Have faith and enjoy

presence in the present, to enjoy everything he has brought to you and be grateful for everything you have.

Being grateful for the small and big things around you also helps you be in a better mood and have a more positive energy every day. It is impossible to focus on the negative or be in a bad mood when you are noticing and being grateful for everything you have. Your thoughts will become more and more positive, and your thinking will be clearer. The more you do it, the easier it will get, the more focused you will be on doing what you are actually able to do to keep moving forward. Negative thoughts will go away, and negative events will disappear from your life. By keeping a positive attitude, you will be in the fast lane to create the life you desire. And if you want to take it up a notch, right after you are grateful for something, say this: Thank you, more of this please. You will open yourself to incredible possibilities that you can't even imagine right now!

Earlier in the book, I talked about an exercise that a friend told me about. To plant seeds of what I truly desired and dreamed of, be thankful for it, and let it grow as long as it needs to. You need to be thankful for what you pray for and plant, just as if you already have it. I tried this exercise many times, and I've always ended up getting what I planted, or even better. It convinced me that in order to achieve the success you desire; you need to be thankful for it as if you already are this successful. Every day, feel the joy and gratefulness that accomplishing this dream will bring you. This will help you feel closer and closer to it until you have it. And before all that, remember to be grateful for what you have and who you are. Then ask for more.

Even though all this gratitude works, not everything will become easy. You will still face tough situations and have difficult moments. It's easy to say, "thank you, God!" after the big win, but gratitude becomes much more difficult during trials. A lot of people start thinking 'Why did this happen to ME? What did I do to deserve this?' That's the wrong approach. Whenever God puts you through difficult times, you need to remember that God loves you and has the best plan for you, even if you don't see it at that time. And perhaps you just need that incident to help you grow into a stronger and better person. Sometimes they are needed to put you on the right track, to help you see your true potential. Even if your circumstances are very difficult, you need to make choices to progress forward, and the first decision is to trust God fully. Keep in mind that He would never give you battles you are not able to win with Him in your corner. Only He truly knows what you are capable of, and He will always be by your side.

I am extremely grateful that you are reading these lines, and I pray to God that he provides me with the right words so that I am able to help you in the best way possible.

Chapter 15

Tool #10

Have faith and enjoy

The final tool! Once you have done everything in your power to achieve a goal, the next very important step is to have faith and be patient. From the moment you enter a race, show or rodeo, you have a certain goal in mind for it. Whether it's to win it or simply improve something, you'll do everything in your power to prepare for it. You feed your horses great nourishment, make sure they are sound and happy, that their shoes are up to date. You ride them to get them in the best physical shape possible and to make sure they are ready to have their best showing. You make sure everything is ready in your trailer, load your horses up and head to the show. Once you get there, you have done everything in your power to get ready to accomplish your goal. When you put the saddle on and go warm your horse up, you have to fully trust all your hard work is going to pay off. This is the moment to show that you have complete faith in God and the efforts you put in. Worrying will not do any good, so have faith in you and your horse. Don't try to change anything at the last minute, be patient, enjoy the ride and go win!

It's the same thing in your life. I can teach you every tool I know, you can read all the books, watch all the motivational videos, and seek many mentors, but if you don't believe that the work, you're putting in will bring the results you want, then you will not get the success you are hoping for.

Whether it's to achieve a goal, change a situation, or get more connected with yourself, once you put the hard work in, it's extremely important to have faith in God and the Universe and know that they are working on it. You cannot control the 'when, why, and how' it will happen. Just remember that it will happen in its time. The timing might not be when you want it to be, but God's timing is perfect. Sometimes, it's later than you expect it, and sometimes it's when you least expect it, but just remember, keep putting the work in, have faith through the entire experience, and everything will work together for your benefit. "All things work together for those who love God" - Romans 8:28 There are many things we do daily where we have faith in the timeline without even thinking about it. The best example is when we go to a restaurant. You enter, take a seat, look at the menu, make a choice and tell the waiter your order. You don't

Have faith and enjoy

question every step, you do it, and then you patiently wait for your waiter to come back with your food. You don't know how long it will exactly take, but you know it's coming. You don't go in the kitchen to see if the cook is doing its job, and you don't change your mind about your choice a million times. You simply know it's getting prepared. It's the same way with God. You look at all the possibilities, identify what you want, take the actions needed to achieve that goal, then you pray about it and have faith that God will create what you desire and have it ready in its perfect timing.

Notice how your emotions and how you are feeling before you even walk in the restaurant can affect your experience. If you walk in happy, you have a lot more patience, even if the wait time is a little longer, or there is a mistake in your order, it's all good. It's not a big deal, it will all work out. On the other hand, if you walk in already in a bad mood, every little thing will bother you, and time will seem to go by a lot slower. If you keep questioning the waiter about everything, or even changing your mind about some things, it will make the process longer and longer. You probably see where I'm going by now. If you keep questioning God's way, or if you don't trust the work you are putting in and keep changing your mind, the process will take longer, and you might not see the results you want to have and when you want to have them. If you have faith, are excited for what's to come and are thankful for it, the entire process will be more joyful, and God will keep the blessings pouring in.

When the restaurant provides you good service, you give the waiter a huge tip to tell them that you're thankful for taking care of you. God's tip is seeing you being successful AND being so thankful and grateful for it, and to see you truly enjoy life.

When you go to a rodeo, show, barrel race, or whatever you are competing in, it's time to fully enjoy the moment and trust that you have done everything in your power to get ready for this moment. There is no training you can do at this point that will make your performance better. Enjoy the ride, work on what needs to improve after. Do not expect the worst, take a deep breath, be present, have faith in you and your horse, and have fun. We do this sport because we love it, right? But we don't usually take time to enjoy it and appreciate the blessing this sport brings. Always remember, that no matter what horse you are getting on, they feel your energy and emotions and feed off that. So, let's show them happiness as much as possible, and give them the confidence to do their best job.

Chapter 16

Straight from the horse's mouth

Horses are magnificent animals capable of teaching us so much. I am privileged to get to listen to them every day and learn "straight from the horse's mouth". I'm blessed to be able to share this knowledge with you, and hopefully it helps you better understand your horse. I'm going to "let the horses talk to you". After communicating with thousands of them, I have heard many common issues. While some have unique circumstances and problems, I found that many problems have similar causes. Horses have, also, taught me a lot about the way they see life and I have learned important lessons from them. They don't get caught up in their head, they keep things simple and live in the present moment. They are herd animals; they focus on trusting their leader and having confidence in them. You are their leader, and if a horse knows he can trust you, at least 90% of them will do their best to please you and listen to you.

If your horse makes a mistake, instead of correcting him immediately, take a second look at how you asked him. How was your body position, your hands and feet placement? Could the cues you gave him sent a mixed signal? They can feel if your body gets slightly tensed, and they understand what you think. So if you think about the problem, or tense your body getting prepared for them to make the said mistake… they most likely will do just that! Your anticipation of a mistake will quickly become what they think is the right way. A horse can feel when your heartbeat gets faster, when you get nervous. They can't always understand why you feel that way, so they get scared, might not want to go in the arena or might not be focused during their run. Their heartbeat will do the same, it creates anxiety for them too. If you have a smartwatch, look at your heart rate and the time it might go up, it might help you get better at controlling it.

Very often, when a horse's performance decreases, there's a reason behind it more than "he's being a jerk". Before going in correction mode, go through a short checklist. Does he have any physical pain? Am I making mistakes while riding? Did I change my cues, and he might not understand it? Do you have some pain that might cause you to ride differently?

For the physical pain, I see a lot of recurring problems while communicating with horses. First thing is their feet. I see a lot of back, SI, hocks, and stifle problems that are created because of the feet. Even if you inject any of them, the soreness always comes back. Working with vets, farriers and the horses, I saw a huge difference when we put all our efforts together for the horses' benefit. It's not just the front feet, you need to take care of the hind feet too. A lot of horses show me the angle. Only 2 degrees on a heel can make a hip sore. Their feet, obviously, hold all their weight, and they can be one of the most sensitive parts. They can feel pressure in their feet and start walking differently to try to release that pressure and be pain free. This can lead to a lot of compensation pain, but it's not always easy to figure out where the pain started, this is why very often, when you inject the feet, you release a lot of back pain. If I've talked with any of your horses, you've probably heard me say this already. I always say that I'm not a vet or a farrier, I just have the chance to work with a lot of them and learn from the best about the physicality of the horse. If your farrier is open to work with the vet, take x-rays of all 4 feet. It will save you a lot of time and money and I promise you; your horse will be happier.

The second most common thing I see is stomach issues. Their stomachs are very sensitive, and many things are prone to creating problems like ulcers. Their nutrition, change in diet, change in temperature, environment, stress, transportation and even some medications can all be things that upset their stomachs. They can all react a different way to the different variables, but they just make me feel what they feel. Sometimes it's ulcers or too much acid and their stomach can be burning, or they can feel car sick. And it's very rarely only the stomach, but the hind gut too. Which can often be forgotten in treatments. Very often, if a horse is not eating well, it's their stomach that is bothering them. If they have some diarrhea, a sensitive flank area, quit running as hard, it's most likely their hind gut. There are a lot of products that work well to treat the stomach, but not nearly as many that take care of the hind gut. If you see/feel any change in your horse and think it could be a stomach/ulcer problem, ask your vet and treat as soon as possible. You won't hurt them by treating it, and it won't heal itself if you don't. One of the main things (if not the thing) that causes ulcers is too much acid in the stomach. I get so many complaints about this from horses, it's absolutely crazy. There are many horses that get car sick. I know this might sound really weird, but it's the best way to explain it. Even if you keep hay in front of them, some horses might still be prone to not feeling good on the trailer. The trailer might cause them some stress or simply the movement on the road causes the acid in their stomach to move around more and make them feel bad. It is not always easy to determine if the stress causes more acid or the acid causes more stress, but one thing is sure, if you don't take care of it, it'll only get worse. What I found to help the most is a pre-race paste given 30-45 minutes before you load them on the trailer. It will coat the inside of the stomach and protect the hind gut, which will protect it all from the burning pain. Some horses start kicking in the trailer, lose weight while on the road, start refusing to get on the trailer, those can all be indicators that their stomach gets upset on the road.

It can be the same before a competition. When horses start to feel stressed, pressure of the competition, sometimes they start having more acid and it creates ulcers. The way I feel those horses is like if they become a dragon in the warm-up pen. Some are more hesitant or refuse to go in the alleyway, or some don't run as hard because their belly hurts. There are a lot of good products on the market to help your horse's gut. When you try something new, keep doing it for 2-3 shows or races because your horse anticipates the pain in their belly. They need to learn that it will be ok and that they are not hurting anymore before you see a change in their behavior. If you don't see any change, try something else. It's not because a product works well on one horse that it will do the same on the others. Every horse reacts differently to products, so figure out what product works best for your horse.

Nutrition is also something horses talk a lot about. They all have different tastes, and their bodies process hay, grain, and supplements differently. To some, grain can be too much, and it can affect their concentration. I like to compare those to kids that you gave a lot of chocolate to, and they are running all over the place. Some supplements can work great with some horses and might not work at all with others. Same with the taste of those supplements. So, when adding something to their diet, do it one thing at a time, and try it for at least a couple of weeks before changing something again. It can take time for them to feel a difference. Plus, if you add many things at once, and they don't like something, there is no way for them to tell exactly which one they don't like. Horses are creatures of habit. I have seen many of them who quit eating because their grain changed so many times or so much at once, that they don't "trust" it anymore, don't feel good about it. The more you are consistent with their food, exercises, and overall routine, the happier they will be and the better results you will get.

I might be stating the obvious here, but their water intake is really important too. Some horses prefer a certain water temperature. I've even seen horses that have preferred bucket colors. So, if they don't drink enough, check all the variables. A lot of people will add electrolyte when it gets hot but stop when it gets cold. That's a mistake because most horses will actually drink less when water is colder. I've seen a lot more horses get dehydrated in the winter than in the summer.

Let's talk about pain. That's a huge part of my work, and usually the reason people call me. Working with vets, chiropractors, farriers, and more, I have learned a lot about it. When I connect with a horse, they don't tell me "Here's where I hurt: right shoulder, left SI, back right coffin". They don't know all these terms. How it works for me is that I feel the pain directly on me. They show me how they feel in their body, so it's like I'm the horse. Very often, they show me the compensation first, rather than where the pain comes from. For example, a lot of people will inject hocks first, but very often they are compensating for something else. The hocks can hold a lot of pressure coming from anywhere else in the body: feet, hips, shoulders, and more. To understand this easily, I compare it to someone breaking a leg;

the broken leg might be painful, but after a while of only walking on the other one, the healthy one might be sorer. If a horse doesn't want to let you pick up a hind leg or wants to put it right back down, in a surprising few situations it is because that leg is hurting. It is usually because they don't want to have to put all the weight on the other hind leg or even on their shoulders. There are many horses that are good for the farrier for their front feet, but hate getting their hind feet done. Why? Their shoulders hurt. Once again, I'm not a vet, but I've seen many situations where horses don't want to get their hind legs manipulated because if they pick them up, it means more weight on the shoulders and it can be very painful.

If you start having problems in competition, you need to look at everything on your horse. I have talked to so many horses that tell me that the rider keeps looking at the same spot over and over because there might have been an injury there in the past, but it is not the problem anymore. It is good sometimes to reset we and forget the past problems and injuries and see things with a renewed perspective. They are real athletes, and they work very hard. So, keep your mind open, and with the right specialists, you can really help them. And please, don't forget the neck, poll and TMJs (temporomandibular or jaw joint). Those are a big part of their body that is often overlooked and can create a lot of issues with the way they react to and work with the bit, move, turn, and it can even affect their behavior. If there is any problem with their poll or TMJs, it can give horses headaches and cause them to move their head weirdly to try to release the pressure, and it can make them act differently too. I'm sure you've had a headache before. It's hard to give your best performance with it. Teeth problems can also be the root of it. A simple fix that is too often forgotten.

Each horse has their own personality. Some like to have fun, some like to work, some need more repetitions/routine, some want to do it all by themselves, and some are the know-it-all type. I know that sometimes, it's hard to know what your horse prefers as a training method. One thing that comes back very often is consistency and simplicity. So, the simpler your cues are, the easier it is for them. When you show them your basic cues, one by one, it is easier for them to follow you afterward, when you ask for more complex things. Some horses don't understand why at home you ask them to work one way, and, in a competition, you are asking so differently. It is good to work on the basics and make sure they remember all the steps during the week, but, once in a while, ride them like you would at a race and let them do their job. No, you do not have to go full speed to do this. Start at a walk, then do it at a trot and a lope if needed. When you school your horse all week, you ask him to wait on you, to follow you. Then at your competition, you sit, and you don't ask for anything. So sometimes horses are like, what the.... I don't understand what (s)he wants, gives me all these million cues at home, but then we get here, I have to do it all myself. So that way, you can feel if your horse understands your cues. Because a lot of them are confused between the training and the race or show.

When a horse knows their basics, knows their job, and doesn't really need any tune-up, many people forget how important it is to still keep them in good shape. And very often horses will even notice that they don't get rode as much and are not in as good of a shape as they used to be. When horses don't get a good amount of exercise, you impair their performance, and increase the chance of injuries. In your training program, think about their lungs. If you just walk them or let them relax all week, many horses will still go give everything they've got in competition and hurt their lungs because they are not used to running that hard. When they bleed or have difficulty breathing, some horses feel more anxiety and refuse to go in the arena. They don't need to bleed out of the nose for that to happen, it can all be internal. The way that I feel it on a horse, it's like if you inhale, and you go underwater at the same time. You will feel like you are drowning, and you might be very stressed because you can't breathe. I'm pretty sure that you will think about it twice before going back in the water. It's the same thing with horses; why would they want to go back in the arena if they are going to live through that again? There are a lot of products, breathing treatments or other solutions that are available to help. The best is to discuss it with your vet. No matter what event you are doing, this is something very important to keep in mind.

The most important point with horses is to keep in mind that they are animals. Yes, they like that you take care of them. Let them roll, play, and enjoy turnout time. Your horse is an animal first, so let them act like one. Don't make them be an athlete all the time. They want to work for you, but they also want to have fun.

They are a gigantic beast with a mind of their own that are doing their best every day to listen to your commands. That's pretty amazing in itself. So, before you get mad at them, remember this and go through the list of everything we've talked about. There is virtually always a good reason that explains their behavior.

Chapter 17

Some remarkable communications

This chapter is all about sharing some real-life stories of a few horses I have communicated with. Unfortunately, for privacy purposes, I cannot mention their names.

— The Mare with the Long Flow —

I talked with a mare that I regularly worked with. The goal with this communication was to make sure she was ready for the National Finals Rodeo. At the end, the rider asked me if the mare felt ready to go. She wasn't really sure what event I was talking about. So, the mare asked me if it was the place where she had a beautiful long tail flowing. Like I told you, I put no doubt in what I received, but it sounds a little bit crazy. So, I repeated what she just said, and they started laughing. The year before, they had put extensions on her tail. So, yes, it was the place! That mare was ready, but she wanted to let them know that she feels very pretty with the long tail flow, and she would love to have it again. They put the extensions back on, naturally. When she was in Vegas, they sent me a video of her walking with her extensions. I can tell you that she was so happy!

— The Bossy Mare —

I talked with a mare that is very, very bossy, "mareish," and who, honestly, does not care about pleasing her owner. She likes to decide everything. The owner called me one day because she had a lot of trouble catching her in the pasture. She even tried to chase her around on the 4-wheeler, hoping the mare would give up, but no success. So, I talked to her and even for me, it was hard to establish a connection with her. She didn't give a shit about me. To be able to establish a connection with her, I had to ask her permission to talk to her. I had to treat her like a queen, like if it was her idea. I talked to the owner and explained it to her. She

Some remarkable communications

needed to ask the mare's permission to catch her, put her blanket on, or whatever else she needed to do with her. It looked like a crazy idea at the beginning, but she went with it and tried it. Since that day, if she wants to catch her, she just asks her permission to do so. And that mare will walk right up to her or do whatever she is asked to because it gives her the choice, forces her to make the decision, puts her in charge, and she feels respected for that.

— A Very Special Mare —

I had a conversation with a three-year-old cutting mare. Even though she was just three, I was feeling something very special about her. She was so smart. She showed me that she liked watching the older horse's work. She was not just watching, but that's how she learned the most. She told me: "I can do what they are doing. Tell my owner that I got this. I'm ready to do more." I explained that to the trainer. I knew her a little bit, but not as a friend, though we have grown to become close friends. She scares me sometimes because she listens to every single thing I say and does it without hesitating, even though I've told her many times that I am not a trainer. She started bringing that mare on the side of the show pen, so she can watch the good horse's work. A few weeks later, she started showing her. She did very well. I can say that I have a real love story with that mare, who is so confident and eager to learn.

— Mares & Ovaries —

I talked with a mare to find out what her issues/pain were. She told me a few things, but the biggest thing was how much her right ovary was bothering her. When I told the owner about all of her pains, they worked on fixing the issues, but didn't pay attention to the ovaries right away. Not long after, the mare started kicking in the trailer and had a very bad attitude. A few weeks later, they took her to the vet again and decided to get her ovaries checked. There was a big cyst on the right one. They fixed it, and she immediately quit kicking in the trailer and went back to her usual demeanor.

— The Connection Between a Rider and a Horse's Bodies —

This horse explained to me that her rider was riding her the opposite way. I really didn't understand what he meant. I thought that maybe when I called the owner, I could talk to her about it, and we could figure it out. I always say that I put no doubt in what I receive, and I promise to the horse to say everything to the owner, even if that could hurt their feelings. I'm there for the horse first. So, I called the owner and told her what her horse told me. She didn't understand either. During phone calls, I always connect to the horse first to make sure that everything I'm saying is accurate and if the person wants to ask more questions, it's possible. While we were trying to understand the horse, he told me, if you want, I can explain to you better when we will be alone. So, I asked the owner for permission to connect with her horse that night, so he can explain it to me. That's what

Some remarkable communications

I did. That night, on my couch, I had a full lesson from a horse on how his body works with how the rider asks. It was amazing. He was saying that she was riding him the opposite way, because during the regular training she asked him to move his shoulder and his hip and move her body the same way. But at the race, to go to the first barrel, she put her right shoulder and hip more in front, because she was pulling on her inside rein and bringing it on the left side of the neck. So, when he arrived at the barrel, his right shoulder and hip were more in front, and that made it hard for him to turn. It was also the same for her two other horses I talked to. After a few hours, I really learned a lot about the connection between the horse and the rider's body. The next morning, I explained to her what the horse taught me that night. She agreed and understood what he wanted to say. I can say that this communication helped her a lot, but it helped me even more.

— A Very Clean Gelding —

It is pretty common to see horses go to, shall we say, excessive lengths to make sure they don't pee on themselves. This horse takes it to another level. To be able to pee, he needs shavings or grass every time to make sure he doesn't splash on himself. He won't even go pee in the trailer because he doesn't have enough space. He was very focused on that when I talked to him, so I told the owner and she started laughing. They were actually on the road at that moment. When he needs to "go" on the road, he starts moving in the trailer so much that she has to pull over to find a spot to let him pee. And that's what he was doing at that very moment of this communication.

Horse Konfidence

— A Gelding with a Very Strong Energy Force —

I was asked to go see this very big gelding I didn't know anything about. When I walked into his stall, I had to take a few steps back because I felt him pushing me away! But it wasn't him walking into me or throwing me away with his nose, it was his energy. He had such a big energy around him, it was so intense. His energy was so powerful, I could feel he was a winner just through his energy. He gave his all, all the time for anything he had to do. He showed me all the prizes he'd won, how much he loved his job, and he made sure to tell me that he did not want to slow down. I was very impressed! That horse was a real champion and the owner confirmed that he won a lot of money. That was the first time that I felt that kind of winning emotion in a horse.

— Studs —

I talk with a lot of studs. People think that they are bossier than any other horses, but in fact, it's not always the case. Usually, mares are very bossy.

I explained to you already that when a horse feels pain or something else, I feel it directly on me. One day, a very well-known trainer asked me to talk with a mare and three of her studs. I did the communication, and after I gave her the results of what I received, she requested I ask the studs if they like to breed. Two of them didn't have a problem with it, it was ok, just part of their job. The last one was another story. He really liked it and was really happy to share that feeling with me. I was so happy to be on the phone so that person could not see my face.

Some remarkable communications

It was something... I even asked her to give me a minute. I had no words to explain it. I was laughing so hard. When I told her that he really enjoyed it, she agreed 100%. That was a weird feeling for me, to say the least.

One of my friends has a stud who had to stay at the breeding farm for a while to quarantine to be able to ship semen to certain countries. The problem was, he hates the stud farm. She asked me to talk to him to tell him what was going to happen and see if there was anything we could do to make his experience better, since during the previous breeding season, he didn't do well staying there. He lost a lot of weight and even hurt himself. He is usually very kind, and he really likes being at home, in his big turn-out where he can see everyone around. The first 2 days in quarantine were ok, but the third day was not good at all. So, I checked up on him. As soon as I connected with him, he was mad, very mad. He told me "I have no friends here. I hate them all." I asked him what we can do to make his life better over there. He told me I need a friend. When I called the owner, I told her it will sound crazy, but if you can bring him a friend, I think he will be better. That's what she did. As soon as his friend arrived, he relaxed, was good for the whole quarantine and was even able to stay there a little longer to have semen collected. I'm so thankful for what the horses tell me, but sometimes even more for the owners' open mind or the specialists that listen and do what I tell them. We all work together to make the horses happier and healthier.

Horse Konfidence

— A Very Smart Horse —

Last year, a friend called me about a horse. He didn't know what to do with him anymore. Every time he brought him in the arena to work, he would buck. The vet looked at him and he was perfectly sound. So, I talked with the horse. He told me that if he was bad, the trainer, instead of fighting with him, would put him in the walker thinking that he would get that bad energy out. That horse preferred the walker. He was smart enough to know that if he tried to buck, he would get to go in the walker. When I called the trainer, I explained to him that he was doing it on purpose because he prefers being on the walker over being ridden. I told him the next time he brought him to the arena, he had to ride him through it. For those who know me, I'm not the kind of person who says to get in a fight and insists with the horse, but in cases like this some horses need it. So, the next day, he brought him to the arena and won the fight, if I can say that. He kept him in the arena until he finally calmed down. He never did that again after that.

— Clones —

I had a chance to talk with three clones. They were all looking the same, and everyone was expecting that they would have the same mindset. I was very impressed that was not the case. Yes, they have the same look, but their personalities are different. Talking with them, I learned a lot of things. They had all the same physical abilities to excel, but the way that they learned and expressed themselves were very different. The interaction that

Some remarkable communications

they had with other horses and humans created their character, too. One of them was very confident, he was a leader, one was just happy and wanted to be good, and the last one was grumpier. When they were born, there's one that was more fragile, so he was handled more and given a lot of health care. That changed his character. The personality of the broodmare plays in, too, to build their character. Every interaction that they had as they grew over time changed their way of evolving mentally. It's a little bit like identical twins. They look the same, but their personalities can be so different. What I saw that day blew my mind.

— Bucking Horses & Bulls —

When I started working with these athletes, it was mostly to find out if they still wanted to buck or not. Then, I got to work with stock contractors to help them find pain on bucking horses before they would take them to the vet to get them injected. Kind of hard to do a proper lameness exam on a wild horse, so it was really awesome to get to help them.

I, now, get to work with the human athletes. Guys will call me to better understand the horse or bull they are about to ride. It amazes me each time. When I talk with them, I feel the animal's energy, and they like to show me what they need to perform better. A mother called me one day and asked me if I could talk with the horse her son drew for a big, short round. When I connected with her, she was very "Show off-ish". She explained to me that her goal is to put on a good show. After two bucks, she usually turns to the right, kicks harder with her back end and decides after that if the guy deserves to stay on her or not. So, I explained that he needs to feel that he's there to make a show with her, not try to dominate her, not be too aggressive, just be there to make her look good and be a little bit show off too. When I saw the video of his ride… wow! It was exactly what she did, two bucks, then turned to the right. And she was putting on a show. Some bucking horses rely more on the cowboy to have a great performance. Some will do the same job no matter what. Some get excited in the chute, while others can get a little aggressive, anxious, or scared. How the competitor handles them in the chute can make a big difference. If a guy is too rough with one, they sometimes get scared, and other times it makes them mad. Some horses like to be reassured in the chute, and some just want the cowboy to be quick and get out of there. I feel so lucky that those professional athletes are open to work with me. They listen to what the horses or bulls have to say, but most importantly, they are working on themselves to have the best mindset for the ride and for the horse. I always love working with animals, but to experience this through coaching these athletes to help them connect with themselves and work with the animals opened up another way to use my gift to help more people to achieve their goals!

Horses have a lot of different personalities and different ways of learning, just like us humans. So, if something works well for a horse, it doesn't mean that it will be the same for others. Very often, after my communication with the horses, their owners call or text me to say that they feel more connected with their horses,

Some remarkable communications

they understand them better and their relationship with them has changed a lot. Just taking time to listen to your horse can make a huge difference on the time you will spend with them. It's not just about the love for a horse, it's about trust, confidence and connection. Never forget that!

It's just the beginning...

My life's purpose has always been to help others, albeit in many various ways. It's only on the day that I really accepted who I am (and I'm still working on it), that my life took a path that I never expected. I know that God still has a lot of surprises planned for me and when they come, I will be ready for them. I will always continue to work on myself to be the best version that I can possibly be. I will continue to be surprised every day that I live. I will always be impressed with each communication with animals. I will always be there to help others. But most importantly now, I will always listen to myself, believe in myself and make choices to achieve my soul's goals!

Everything started with a dream, an idea, a feeling. Three years ago, I had this crazy idea of writing a book in English, even if I'm not a writer and my English is still far from perfect. I started asking questions to God, the Universe, not having a doubt on what I received and doing some research to find a way to realize it. It was not that easy, and sometimes I almost quit. But I was always asking questions to find the right way to make this happen and to achieve my goal to help more people and animals. The answer was always "YES". So, I never quit.

I hope this book will help you, too, in your life. At the same time, it was a good reminder for me. There's always something to learn, to grow, and to achieve. I believe it's life's purpose. I know that I will live a very long life... I still have so much to do, to learn, and to be, and I'm pretty sure that I will still receive some other crazy ideas. But I can promise you one thing, I will continue to enjoy every second of it and be proud of what I've done, and what I will accomplish.

I wish you all the same, because life can be so much fun!

With infinite gratitude,

Katheleen

Testimonials

"Katheleen possesses an innate gift that gives us an insight and understanding to our horse's souls. I have had the pleasure of working with her on multiple horses, and her insight allows me to treat horses whose issues have been harder to pinpoint. It is evident that Kathleen's mission in life is to utilize her gift to help as many horses and owners as possible."

    Zach Bruggen, DVM

"I met Katheleen through my vet, Molly Bellefeuille, about two years ago. She is truly a gift from God to my program! If she tells me something- I DO IT! We have trained several successful horses together. I've been cutting for 20 years and in the last two I doubled my lifetime earnings, won 3 futurity jackets, & got inducted into the non pro hall of fame! My motto is I have God & Katheleen!"

    Missy Jean Etheridge

"Katheleen and I have done a lot of work together in terms of different diagnostics and different treatment methods in order to see some of the things that we're doing to treat these horses. Even as a veterinarian, Katheleen has helped open my eyes to things that by no means can I communicate with the horse. But there's things that she's shown me to open my eyes to where I can notice and understand them a little bit better into how they work and how they think and stuff like that from a vet point to try to make these horses feel better and treat some of the things that they have going on with them."

    Dr. Clay Espy

"Working with Katheleen has completely changed my perspective on the importance of listening to your horse and my ability to do so. She's helped me immensely with my confidence and taught me how to feed that confidence into my horses. I can't imagine not having Kathleen in my corner."

    Paris Jean

"We've used her in our operation for the last four years since she's come here from Canada, and we've had lots of success with her. One of the reasons that we like Katheleen to work with the horses is it gives us a different thought process on how our horses actually think and get us to connect with our horses a little more."

    Dustin Angelle

Testimonials

"Working with Katheleen I am able to help my horses feel good, be the best they can be and perform at the top level."

    Shali Nicols Lord

"Katheleen helped me on my journey and my horses. We have been working together for probably four years or so, on a lot of horses. Whether it's mental, riding, health, just all the things she's helped me with. She would come and communicate with my horses and help me figure out stuff that I or vets or chiropractors or whoever couldn't figure out. Then, mentally, she helped me a lot just bond with the horses and believe in myself, mostly in pretty extreme and very high-pressure situations. She helps me keep my nerves down and keep focus, and just reach a lot of goals that I don't think would have been attainable without her help.

Not only has she helped me get the horses to that level, but me personally in my competition and just believe in myself to get me there. I think that this book will help people not only get there themselves, but everybody. There's just so much that she brings to the table with her gifts and being able to communicate with horses, but also being able to help people and their horses get to that next level as well."

    Tasha Welsh

To watch the full version of these interviews in video, visit www.horsekonfidence.com/bookgift

FREE GIFT

Practice the tools to improve your life NOW!

To thank you for taking the time to read this book, I have prepared a secret video for you, along with a downloadable exercise guide to help you implement the tools in your life, right away.

You can get it all for free, simply by entering your email address here:

https://www.horsekonfidence.com/bookgift

About the Author

Katheleen moved to the United States about 4 years ago from Thetford Mines, Quebec, Canada, to fully concentrate on communicating with animals. Living all her life in a French-speaking province, it was quite the challenge to move to Texas with these southerners and their million slang terms and make the switch to speaking English every day. With a remarkable 23 years of teaching experience, she now helps horse trainers and horse lovers to better understand their horses regarding their health, training, and happiness.

Because of her inborn passion for animals, she decided to establish Horse Konfidence so that she could broaden her horizons and meet with more people to help work towards her main goal: the well-being of animals.

Since she has been given the gift to naturally understand horses, she has been able to understand and feel what they have to say. A lot of the horses have talked to Katheleen about how they feel about their rider, what stresses them, their pains and more. She wants to help horses, their riders, and owners as much as she can. Hence, she decided that sharing her knowledge, experience, and tools is the best way to attain this goal. With this book, she hopes to help people understand themselves better and be able to connect with their horses more so that they can become a better team!

www.ingramcontent.com/pod-product-compliance
Lightning Source LLC
Chambersburg PA
CBHW060524090426
42735CB00011B/2357